Charles Dickens's
GREAT EXPECTATIONS

Bloom's NOTES

A CONTEMPORARY
LITERARY VIEWS BOOK

Edited and with an Introduction by
HAROLD BLOOM

© 1996 by Chelsea House Publishers, a subsidiary of Haights Cross Communications.

Introduction © 1996 by Harold Bloom

Printed and bound in the United States of America.

3 5 7 9 8 6 4 2

Library of Congress Cataloging-in-Publication Data

Charles Dickens' Great expectations / edited and with an introduction by Harold Bloom.
p.   cm. — (Bloom's Notes)
Includes bibliographical references.
ISBN 0-7910-3659-6
1. Dickens, Charles, 1812-1870. Great expectations. I. Bloom, Harold.
II. Series: Bloom, Harold. Bloom's Notes.
PR4560.C43 1996
823'.8—dc20
95-13560
CIP

Chelsea House Publishers
1974 Sproul Road, Suite 400
P.O. Box 914
Broomall, PA 19008-0914

Contents

User's Guide

This volume is designed to present biographical, critical, and bibliographical information on Charles Dickens and *Great Expectations.* Following Harold Bloom's introduction, there appears a detailed biography of the author, discussing the major events in his life and his important literary works. Then follows a thematic and structural analysis of the work, in which significant themes, patterns, and motifs are traced. An annotated list of characters supplies brief information on the chief characters in the work.

A selection of critical extracts, derived from previously published material by leading critics, then follows. The extracts consist of statements by the author on his work, early reviews of the work, and later evaluations down to the present day. The items are arranged chronologically by date of first publication. A bibliography of Dickens's writings (including a complete listing of all books he wrote, cowrote, edited, and translated in his lifetime, and important posthumous publications), a list of additional books and articles on him and on *Great Expectations,* and an index of themes conclude the volume.

Harold Bloom is Sterling Professor of the Humanities at Yale University and Henry W. and Albert A. Berg Professor of English at the New York University Graduate School. He is the author of twenty books and the editor of more than thirty anthologies of literature and literary criticism.

Professor Bloom's works include *Shelley's Mythmaking* (1959), *The Visionary Company* (1961), *Blake's Apocalypse* (1963), *Yeats* (1970), *A Map of Misreading* (1975), *Kabbalah and Criticism* (1975), and *Agon: Towards a Theory of Revisionism* (1982). *The Anxiety of Influence* (1973) sets forth Professor Bloom's provocative theory of the literary relationships between the great writers and their predecessors. His most recent books are *The American Religion* (1992) and *The Western Canon* (1994).

Professor Bloom earned his Ph.D. from Yale University in 1955 and has served on the Yale faculty since then. He is a 1985 MacArthur Foundation Award recipient and served as the Charles Eliot Norton Professor of Poetry at Harvard University in 1987–88. He is currently the editor of the Chelsea House series Major Literary Characters and Modern Critical Views, and other Chelsea House series in literary criticism.

Introduction

HAROLD BLOOM

Charles Dickens reread his autobiographical novel, *David Copperfield,* before he began to write *Great Expectations.* He hoped thus not to repeat himself, and his hope was fulfilled: David and Pip are very different personages. Yet Dickens's anxiety was justified; both of these first-person narrators are versions of Dickens himself, and only acute self-awareness on the novelist's part kept Pip from becoming as autobiographical a figure as David had been. Still, one can wonder whether Pip is not a better representation of Dickens's innermost being than David is. Compared to Pip's incessant and excessive sense of guilt, David's consciousness seems much freer, or at least works in a more unimpeded fashion to liberate itself, in part, from the personal past. Pip does not become a novelist, as David and Dickens do, and Pip also does not submit to sentimentality, as David does. We are asked to believe that David Copperfield concludes the novel as a fully matured being, but we are left with considerable doubts. Pip, perhaps because he is more distanced from Dickens, seems more worthy of Dickens's respect and is endowed by the novelist with a more powerful imagination than the novelist David Copperfield enjoys.

Why does Pip have so pervasive a sense of guilt? Several critics have remarked that, in Pip, love always emanates from guilt, whether the love be for the father-substitutes Joe and Magwitch, or the overwhelming passion for the beautiful, mocking, and unattainable Estella. Dickens's best biographer, Edgar Johnson, relates this erotic aspiration to the novelist's love affair with Ellen Ternan, an actress quite young enough to have been his daughter.

Since Estella actually is Magwitch's daughter, and Magwitch has adopted Pip as a son, pragmatically speaking, there is something of an incest barrier between Pip and Estella, though Pip consciously cannot be aware of this. And yet he is conscious that she is "part of my existence, part of myself": there is as occult a connection between Pip and Estella as there is between Heathcliff and the first Catherine in Emily Brontë's *Wuthering Heights.* One critic, Shuli Barzilai, relates Pip's self-lacerating temperament to Freud's "moral masochism," the guilty need to fail, and she traces the same self-punishing pattern in Estella's marriage to the sadistic Bentley Drummle. Both Estella and Pip seem doomed to go on expiating a guilt not truly their own, whether or not it was truly Charles Dickens's.

Dickens originally ended the novel with a powerful unhappiness: Pip and Estella meet by chance in London; she has remarried, and each sees in the other a suffering that cannot be redressed. Unfortunately, Dickens revised this into the present conclusion, in which Pip prophesies that he and Estella will not be parted again. Though this is a little ambiguous and just evades sentimentality, it is highly inappropriate to what is most wonderful about the novel: The purgation, through acceptance of loss, that has carried Pip into an authentic maturity. What matters in that maturation is not that guilt has been evaded or transcended, but that the reader has come to understand it, however implicitly, as the cost of Pip's confirmation as an achieved self. What Dickens could not bring himself to do in *David Copperfield,* he disciplined himself into doing in *Great Expectations.* Self-made, even self-fathered, Dickens disowns part of that psychic achievement when he creates Pip, who is fatherless but keeps faith at last both with Joe and with the memory of Magwitch. ❖

Biography of
Charles Dickens

Charles John Huffam Dickens was born in Landport, Portsea, near Portsmouth, England, on February 7, 1812, the second of eight children of John and Elizabeth Barrow Dickens. The family moved to London in 1814, to Chatham in 1817, and then back to London in 1822. By 1824 increasing financial difficulties caused Dickens's father to be briefly imprisoned for debt; Dickens himself was put to work for a few months at a shoe-blacking warehouse. Memories of this painful period in his life were to influence much of his later writing, in particular the early chapters of *David Copperfield.*

After studying at the Wellington House Academy in London (1824–27), Dickens worked as a solicitor's clerk (1827–28), then worked for various newspapers, first the *True Sun* (1832–34) and later, as a political reporter, for the *Morning Chronicle* (1834–36). In 1833 Dickens fell in love with Maria Beadnell, but her family opposed any contemplated marriage. Dickens never forgot Maria, and she served as the model for Dora in *David Copperfield.*

In 1836 a collection of articles contributed to various periodicals appeared in two volumes as *Sketches by "Boz," Illustrative of Every-day Life and Every-day People.* This was followed by the enormously popular *Posthumous Papers of the Pickwick Club* (1836–37). Like many of Dickens's later novels, the *Pickwick Papers* first appeared in a series of monthly chapbooks or "parts." Other novels were serialized in magazines before appearing in book form. In 1836 Dickens married Catherine Hogarth, with whom he had ten children before their separation in 1858. At the beginning of his marriage, Catherine's sixteen-year-old sister Mary lived with them, but she died after a few months. The shock of this loss affected Dickens permanently, and Mary would be the model for many of the pure, saintly heroines in his novels—such as Little Nell in *The Old Curiosity Shop*—who die at an early age.

Between 1837 and 1839 Dickens published a second novel, *Oliver Twist,* in monthly installments in *Bentley's Miscellany,* a new periodical of which he was the first editor. This was followed in 1838–39 by *Nicholas Nickleby*. Dickens then founded his own weekly, *Master Humphrey's Clock* (1840–41), in which appeared his novels *The Old Curiosity Shop* and *Barnaby Rudge*. In 1842 he and his wife visited the United States and Canada, and after returning home Dickens published *American Notes* (1842), two volumes of impressions that caused much offense in the United States. He then wrote *Martin Chuzzlewit* (1843–44), a novel set partly in America.

In 1843 Dickens published *A Christmas Carol*, the first in a series of Christmas books that included *The Chimes* (1845), *The Cricket on the Hearth* (1846), *The Battle of Life* (1846), and *The Haunted Man and the Ghost's Bargain* (1848). Early in 1846 he was for a brief time the editor of the *Daily News*, a paper of the Radical party to which he contributed "Pictures of Italy" after visiting Italy in 1844 and again in 1845. During a visit to Switzerland in 1846 Dickens wrote his novel *Dombey and Son*, which appeared monthly between 1846 and 1848. In 1850 he started the periodical *Household Words*; in 1859 it was incorporated into *All the Year Round*, which Dickens continued to edit until his death. Much of his later work was published in these two periodicals, including *David Copperfield* (1849–50), *Bleak House* (1852–53), *Hard Times* (1854), *Little Dorrit* (1855–57), *A Tale of Two Cities* (1859), *Great Expectations* (1860–61), and *Our Mutual Friend* (1864–65).

Throughout his life, Dickens threw himself vigorously into a variety of social and political crusades, such as prison reform, improvement of education, the status of workhouses, and reform of the copyright law (American publishers were notorious for pirating his works and offering him no compensation). These interests find his way also into his work, which is characterized by sympathy for the oppressed and a keen examination of class distinctions. His novels and stories have been both praised and censured for their sentimentality and their depiction of "larger-than-life" characters, such as Pickwick or Mr. Micawber (in *David Copperfield*).

During the last twenty years of his life Dickens still found time to direct amateur theatrical productions, sometimes of his own plays. He also became involved in a variety of philanthropical activities, gave public readings, and in 1867–68 visited America for a second time. Dickens died suddenly on June 9, 1870, leaving unfinished his last novel, *The Mystery of Edwin Drood,* which was first published later that same year. Several editions of his collected letters have been published. Despite his tremendous popularity during and after his own life, it was not until the twentieth century that serious critical study of his work began to appear. Modern critical opinion has tended to favor the later, more somber and complex works over the earlier ones characterized by boisterous humor and broad caricature. ❖

Thematic and Structural Analysis

Great Expectations is in many ways typical of Charles Dickens's numerous novels. It is narrated in an exuberant and verbally playful style. It teems with a wide variety of odd, obsessive, wonderfully vivid characters. In mood, it runs the full range from hilarity to sentimental tenderness to merciless satire to gothic melodrama and violence to crime-fiction suspense. It describes village, town, and city life. It portrays the upper, middle, and lower classes, including the criminal underworld. It probes the deepest loves and fears, hopes and disappointments of a maturing boy. And it offers a dark vision of the psychological effects of the particular kind of class-society fostered by industrial capitalism in nineteenth-century England. Yet *Great Expectations* is atypical of Dickens's work in that it manages to contain all this within a relatively economical plot. Unlike many of Dickens's more diffuse, open-ended narratives, *Great Expectations* is carefully organized so that at each new turn of events the main character and narrator, Philip Pirrip (Pip), learns more about himself by learning more about the complex social web in which he is enmeshed.

We first meet Pip, in **chapter one**, out in the "marsh country" near the small cottage where he lives with his shrewish and abusive older sister, "Mrs. Joe," and her husband, "Joe," a kind and gentle blacksmith. As the young Pip ponders the gravestones of his parents and his five siblings, he is seized by "a fearful man" wearing a great iron chain around his leg. The man picks Pip up, turns him upside down, and shakes him until his pockets are emptied. In a terrifying voice, he threatens to tear Pip's heart and liver out unless he promises to get him a file and some food. After swearing to do so, Pip runs home, and on the following day he fulfills his promise by bringing the convict his own uneaten dinner from the night before, as well as a variety of nutritious goodies pinched from Mrs. Joe's pantry and a file from Joe's forge. The convict thanks Pip, and sets out in pursuit of another convict Pip had spotted on the marshes. "I'll pull him down like a bloodhound," the first convict growls as he departs.

The next day is Christmas, and Pip's guilt and anxiety rise rapidly as he realizes that the brandy and pork pie he gave to the convict were intended for Mrs. Joe's big holiday dinner. She has invited the big-voiced, bald-headed church clerk Mr. Wopsle, the "sawdusty" wheelwright Mr. Hubble, and Joe's uncle Mr. Pumblechook—a pompous and longwinded corn-chandler given to holding forth on the natural viciousness of children. They arrive and sit down to eat (**chapter two**), and conversation turns as usual to a litany of Pip's crimes and the countless inconveniences he causes. "I was always treated," Pip observes comically, "as if I had insisted on being born in opposition to the dictates of reason, religion, and morality, and against the dissuading arguments of my best friends." Only Joe makes any effort to support Pip. In a gesture characteristic of his quiet kindness, Joe silently spoons gravy from his own onto Pip's plate as the other adults lecture the child. Pip manages to endure the first course by clutching the leg of the table, but when Pumblechook gags on the tar-water Pip has substituted for the brandy he took for the convict, and Mrs. Joe calls for the missing pork-pie, Pip's guilty fears overcome him and he bolts for the door.

At the doorway, however, Pip runs headlong into a group of soldiers who have come to enlist Joe's help "in his majesty's service" (**chapter five**). Attention is diverted from dinner as the soldiers tell of the escaped convicts they are chasing, and Joe fires up the forge to repair a set of handcuffs. When the soldiers set out again in pursuit, Joe takes Pip on his back and they follow, but Joe confides to Pip that he hopes the convicts get away. Pip is principally concerned that the convict will believe that he (Pip) has brought the soldiers to him. But his worries prove unfounded when they catch up to the convicts grappling at the bottom of a ditch. Pip's convict explains that he could have escaped, but he could not bear to let the other escaped prisoner go free. He also apologizes to Joe, and protects Pip by explaining that it was he, the convict, who stole the food fron Mrs. Joe's pantry. Joe, typically, does not begrudge the prisoner food and aid. "Poor, miserable, fellow creature," he says compassionately, as he and Pip watch the ragged and bloodied men being led towards the prison ship.

Upon returning to the house and the forge in **chapter seven**, Pip begins to feel guilty about his collusion with the convict. He does not mind having put one over on Mrs. Joe, but towards Joe he feels the deepest affection and friendship. Joe is both Pip's playmate and protector. He does what he can to shield Pip from the violent wrath of Mrs. Joe, and he takes every opportunity to join in Pip's childish pleasures. They share a kind of private language that enables them to sustain a sense of fun in defiance of Mrs. Joe's grim regime—silently comparing the size of their slices of bread, for example, as they chew through them before dinner. "What larks!", Joe often says to Pip as he grows older, poignantly reminding him of their happier moments of spontaneous mischief. "I loved Joe," the narrator reflects, "perhaps for no better reason in those early days than that the poor dear fellow let me love him." He thus feels particularly "cowardly" for not being able to tell Joe about the file he stole from the forge. But his awareness of his weakness does not allow him to overcome it. Indeed, remaining silent about the file is only the first in a long series of disloyalties to Joe that forms the most painful part of Pip's moral education.

The next phase of this education begins in **chapter eight** when Pip receives a communication from Miss Havisham—"an immensely rich and grim lady who lived in a large and dismal house barricaded against robbers, and who led a life of seclusion." She requests that Pip provide her some diversion in her loneliness by playing at her house. Hopeful that Miss Havisham might eventually "do something" to help Pip advance in society, Mrs. Joe cleans him up, stuffs him into "[his] tightest and fearfullest suit," and sends him off. Miss Havisham, Pip discovers, is extremely eccentric; despite her very advanced years, she dresses as if she were a bride—all in white, including a veil and bridal flowers. The whites are yellowing and brittle with age, however, and all the clocks in the room are stopped at exactly twenty to nine. She explains to Pip that she has not seen daylight since before he was born, and he later finds out that she has neither changed her clothes, nor wound the clocks, nor altered any detail since the wedding day many years ago when the groom jilted her. Her only interest is to train Estella (the young girl who lives with her) to take revenge upon all males.

Estella wastes no time in starting in on Pip. As they dutifully play cards under the haggard eye of Miss Havisham, Estella viciously mocks Pip for his uncouth language, his "coarse" hands, and his "thick" boots. The insults sting sharply, not only because Pip had fallen hopelessly in love with Estella immediately upon seeing her, but also because it is the first time that anyone has ever made him conscious that his origins are "common."

The shame and self-hatred that Pip "catches" here from Estella lie at the dark psychological core of Dickens's novel. Above all else, *Great Expectations* is a book about social class. More specifically, it is about how in a class-based society such as that of Victorian England class discriminations seep into and contaminate the deepest and subtlest levels of human feeling and motivation. From the moment that Estella disdains Pip as a "common laboring boy," Pip's feelings and attitudes toward things are fundamentally altered. He begins to have new ambitions for book learning and correct speech. He becomes self-conscious about clothing and appearances. He begins to feel ambivalent about the prospect of following a career as a blacksmith. He becomes critical of the rough casualness of his rural surroundings. And most damaging, he loses the capacity for spontaneous uncritical intimacy with his closest companion, Joe. "I wished Joe had been rather more genteelly brought up," he reflects, "and then I should have been so, too." At all these levels and others, Pip's attitudes come to be shaped by the class divisions which structure his society as a whole. To reveal this painful process to the eyes of his readers was perhaps Dickens' principal thematic aim in writing *Great Expectations.*

Soon after returning to the village from Miss Havisham's, Pip initiates an ambitious program for making himself into "a gentleman." He enlists the aid of Biddy, a wise and kindly relative of Mr. Wopsle, to help expand his knowledge and improve his manners. He applies himself earnestly to Biddy's lessons and seems to himself to be improving until one night when he goes to fetch Joe from the pub on his way home from school (**chapter ten**). A stranger in the pub seems to recognize Pip and nods at him. Pip declines the stranger's offer of a seat next to him, in favor of his customary place next to Joe. The stranger then takes up conversation with Joe about the recently captured "vagrants" in the marsh country, all the while rubbing his leg in an odd and portentous way. As Joe explains that he was only involved in the chase as an onlooker, the stranger orders drinks and makes sure that Pip sees as he slowly mixes his drink with a file—the same file that Pip took from Joe's forge. Much to Pip's relief, Joe soon gets up to leave, but before they go, the stranger gives Pip a shilling wrapped in some crumbled pieces of paper. When he gets home Pip realizes that the pieces of paper are actually two one-pound notes. Joe races back to the pub to try to return them, but the stranger has already left. It is clear to Pip that the stranger in the bar is somehow connected to the convict he assisted, but it is consistent with his ambitions that he now feels sullied rather than honored by the convict's gratitude. He worries about what Estella might think of his connection to this "low" personage, and he has nightmares in which the file comes menacingly toward him.

Pip's aspirations toward gentility are further checked in **chapter eleven** when Miss Havisham offers to purchase his "indentures," thereby making him legally an apprentice to Joe. This transaction requires that Joe come to Miss Havisham's house, and Pip finds himself deeply embarrassed by Joe's ill-fitting Sunday clothes and bashful manners. "I am afraid I was ashamed of the good dear fellow," the narrator recalls, "when I saw Estella's eyes laughing mischeviously." For Joe and the people in the village the securing of the apprenticeship is a cause for celebration, but for Pip it is only a sad reminder of the distance between his world and that of Estella. Because of Joe, the narrator reflects, he had once held the profession of blacksmith sacred, but now it seems "coarse and common." He is constantly fearful as he works at his chores that Estella will look in the window and see him covered in grime and soot. It is only his lingering affection for Joe that keeps him from running away. "It is not possible to know how far the influence of any amiable honest-hearted duty-doing man flies out into the world, but it is very possible to know how it has touched one's self in going by, and I know that any good that intermixed itself with my apprenticeship came of plain contented Joe, and not of restless aspiring, discontented me."

Pip perseveres in this ambivalent way over the next four years. He continues to educate himself with Biddy's help, and the hope that Miss Havisham will eventually make his fortune sustains him. But when he visits Miss Havisham on his birthday she tells him that Estella has been sent away to Europe to be trained "for a lady," and that she herself will do nothing further for him. The only event that breaks the monotony of life in the village is the bludgeoning of Mrs. Joe. Upon returning from town on one occasion (**chapter fifteen**), Pip finds out that Mrs. Joe has been knocked down and nearly killed by a tremendous blow to the head. The only evidence on the scene is a convict's leg-iron. Pip of course immediately feels guilty that he may have contributed to the crime by helping to liberate the perpetrator. But the more likely suspect is Orlick—a morose and powerful journeyman blacksmith's assistant who had been defeated in a fight with Joe over his preferential treatment of Pip a few days before the crime. Orlick of course denies any involvement, and provides a viable alibi. His story is further supported when Mrs. Joe, now speechless and immobile, manages to communicate approval of Orlick from her sickbed.

The mystery remains unsolved, and it is soon forgotten when, in **chapter eighteen**, an assertive, imposing, "bullying" sort of man by the name of Jaggers arrives to tell Pip that he has "great expectations"—that he has "come into a handsome property," and that he will be brought up a gentleman. The only conditions are that Joe release Pip from his "indentures," that his benefactor remain a secret, and that Pip agree always to be called Pip. Much to the man's surprise, Joe agrees immediately to release Pip, and is offended by the idea that he might want some financial compensation for granting his young friend's freedom. With this matter settled, Jaggers informs Pip that a man by the name of Matthew Pocket will be his tutor, and that he, Jaggers, will be his guardian. Pip is to purchase some suitable clothes, and come to London as soon as possible, where Jaggers will assist him in finding lodgings.

Pip's remarkable good fortune goes immediately to his head (**chapter nineteen**). As he prepares to leave, he looks with condescension on everyone and everything in the village. He takes comfort in the thought that his association with the convict on the marshes will now be left far behind him. He asks Biddy to help Joe while he is gone "with his learning and with his manners." When Biddy gently suggests that Joe might be too "proud" to allow himself to be "improved" in this way, Pip decides she must be jealous of his advantages. He allows himself to be fawned over by the tailor, and he warms toward the previously hated Mr. Pumblechook, who is appropriately obsequious. He even insists on being allowed to walk out of the village alone in his new clothes because he is worried that Joe's rough presence might ruin the effect. He only softens when he looks behind him to see that Joe and Biddy are throwing old shoes in his wake and cheering in the traditional manner of folk farewells.

Pip's passage from the country to the city is significant both as a decisive stage in his own personal history, and as a marker of an important feature of the sociological landscape of Victorian England. In moving away from the village world of Joe and Biddy and Mr. Wopsle, Pip leaves behind a stable, deeply rooted, traditional community where everyone was known and where the home and the workplace were often close by and integrated. Arriving in London, he encounters an anonymous, quickly changing, unfamiliar world of transients and hard-nosed professionals for whom work life and home life are sharply separated. Where physical strength, manual know-how, and the familiar were valued in the village, abstract knowledge, professional prestige, and money are valued in the city. This contrast in value-systems is rendered most vividly in Pip's encounters with the lawyer Mr. Jaggers and his assistant Mr. Wemmick (**chapter twenty**). Jaggers and Wemmick are incarnations of professionalism. Unlike easy-going and affectionate Joe, they are abrupt, impersonal, officious, and always on a schedule. And unlike passive and fatalistic Joe, they are aggressive, efficient, and effective. For them, time is money. And money, or, as Wemmick calls it, "portable property," is all-important. Their speech is filled with legal terminology and phrasing. They refuse to allow any hint of sentiment to cloud their strictly rational behavior. Only when he has an opportunity to visit Wemmick at home and to see his indulgent treatment of his aged father does Pip get to see the softer, more spontaneous side of his personality. And Wemmick takes every precaution to ensure that no hint of these "private and personal" weaknesses are carried into his professional sphere. He has a moat built around his home, and he crosses into it by means of a drawbridge. Jaggers, similarly, washes his hands compulsively after every meeting with a client, and does his best never to let on that he is often motivated by generous impulses. His profession so thoroughly dominates his personality that even those who are invited to dine with him at home go away feeling as if they have been on trial.

Happily for Pip, Jaggers and Wemmick are not the only people he meets in London. The tutor to whom Jaggers assigns him, Mr. Matthew Pocket, is kind and helpful, and Pip is assigned to take up lodging with his son Herbert (**chapter twenty-two**). As it turns out, Pip had already met Herbert in the courtyard of Miss Havisham's house. At that time Herbert had presented himself as an upper-class rival for Estella's affections, and Pip had responded to his challenge to fight by knocking him down several times. But Herbert has conveniently misremembered the incident as his own victory, and he apologizes to Pip for bloodying his nose. Pip is instantly charmed by the courteousness and innocence of Herbert's manner, and they soon develop a warm and sincere friendship. There was, the narrator recalls, "a frank and easy way about Herbert that was very taking"; he seemed to have "a natural incapacity to do anything secret or mean." Herbert coaches Pip on table manners with such subtle tact that Pip is never embarrassed, and when the opportunity later presents itself, Pip draws upon his new-found fortune to give Herbert a start in business. They also confide in each other about their respective romantic frustrations; Pip supports Herbert's efforts to marry Clara, a decent and good-hearted girl whom his mother sees as socially "beneath" him, while Herbert attempts to warn Pip away from Estella, whom he describes as "hard, haughty, and capricious in the last degree." He also enlightens Pip to some extent about her history. She was adopted, Herbert tells him, after a suitor not only broke Miss Havisham's heart, but also managed to obtain the ownership of her family's brewery.

Unfortunately, Pip's friendship with Herbert is one of the only redeeming features of the first part of his career in London. He does apply himself diligently to the books Mr. Pocket assigns him, but for the most part, it is a period of callow and irresponsible adolescence (**chapters twenty-four through thirty-four**). The generous allowance which Jaggers gives him from his anonymous benefactor allows Pip to run up large debts. He hires a servant, decorates his rooms lavishly, dines expensively, dresses exquisitely, and in general puts on the airs of a gentleman. He involves himself in a young men's club entitled "The Finches of the Grove" whose members do little but drink and insult one another. Pip generally gets the worst of it in these exchanges from a high-born loafer by the name of Bentley Drummle, whom he describes as "idle, proud, niggardly, reserved, and suspicious." Pip courts Estella slavishly when she returns from Europe, but Bentley Drummle bests him in this sphere as well, as Miss Havisham recognizes the advantages of Drummle's family wealth and connections. And to complete his unhappiness and disorientation, Pip does little to maintain contact with Joe, Biddy, and the village. On the one occasion when Joe does visit London (**chapter twenty-seven**), he is hopelessly self-conscious and out of place at Pip's sophisticated table, and Pip finds himself irritated and embarassed. Joe leaves quickly, but in one of the novel's saddest moments, he first pauses to acknowledge the disruption of their former intimacy: "Divisions among such must come, and must be met as they come. . . . You and me is not two figures to be together in London; nor yet anywhere else but what is private, and known, and understood among friends. . . . I'm wrong in these clothes, I'm wrong out of the forge, the kitchen, or off the meshes."

Pip does return briefly to the forge and the kitchen not long after, on the occasion of Mrs. Joe's death (**chapter thirty-five**). The wounds inflicted by the unknown assailant finally kill her, and Pip is jostled by conflicting emotions of guilt and relief as he confronts mortality close up for the first time. He dines after the funeral with Biddy and Joe, but their relations remain strained by formality. On an after-dinner walk Biddy accurately doubts Pip's promises to come back and see Joe regularly. As he leaves, Pip is pained to see Joe attempt to wipe the coal from off of his hand before he shakes hands with his now genteel former companion.

These pangs are forgotten upon Pip's return to London in the excitement of his official "coming of age" in **chapter thirty-six**. Upon turning twenty-one, Pip reports to Mr. Jaggers as requested, full of expectation that the name of his benefactor will be revealed. He is certain that it must be Miss Havisham, and hopeful that permission to marry Estella will be the reward of his maturity. He is disappointed, however, to find Jaggers his usual, reserved and cryptic self. He merely questions Pip accusingly about his accumulated debts, and gives him a five-hundred-pound bank-note, which, he is told, he will hereafter receive yearly.

It is not until two years later that Pip discovers, to his great shock, the identity of the person who has so generously sponsored him. Herbert Pocket is away on business for the firm in which Pip has helped to establish him, and Pip is sitting quietly reading on a rainy night in their new flat, when he hears footsteps on the stairway (**chapter thirty-nine**). A voice requests Pip by name. When he opens the door, Pip finds a weathered, aging, and unkempt but muscular man with a happy look of recognition on his face walking up toward him with his two hands outstretched in welcome. Pip recoils in horror three times from this most ungentlemanly figure, until he at last recognizes him as the convict from long ago on the marshes, and reluctantly takes his hands. The man kisses them, proclaiming: "You acted nobly, my boy! Noble Pip! And I have never forgot it." Still reluctant, Pip allows the man in and offers him a drink and a place by the fire, where the man sits and tells his extraordinary story. His name, Pip learns, is Abel Magwitch, and not long after his encounter with Pip on the marshes he was banished for life to Australia. There he reformed and applied himself to honest business and became hugely successful in sheep farming, stock trading, and a variety of other occupations. His sole motivation in all his increasingly profitable endeavors, he explains to Pip, was to make a gentleman out of the little blacksmith's boy who had once come to his aid. So with the help of Mr. Jaggers, who had once been his lawyer, he contributed all of his extra money toward that purpose, and the books on Pip's walls, Pip's elegant rooms, Pip's fine clothes, and Pip's superior accent are all gratifying evidence that Magwitch succeeded. "You see," he tells Pip, "I'm your second father. I've made a gentleman of you! Its me wot has done it. I lived rough, that you should live smooth. I worked hard that you should be above work."

For Pip there is nothing gratifying about Magwitch's disclosures. On the contrary, they represent the final dashing of all of his illusions. Miss Havisham, it is now certain, has no further intentions toward him. Estella is surely not designed for him. And, most painful of all, it is now clear that he abandoned Joe not for a higher social station, but for an illegal alliance with a criminal. This criminal, Pip also learns, is in great danger, because the penalty for returning to England after banishment is death. So Pip is not only saddled with the affectionate presence of a man of whom he is ashamed and frightened, but he must also find a way to protect this man, and perhaps to help him escape. In the process of doing so, Pip discovers that he is not the only person who was unknowingly connected to the underworld.

Soon after Herbert Pocket returns, Magwitch supplies them with a full account of his life up until his meeting on the marshes with Pip (**chapter forty-two**). His orphaned childhood was devoted to bare survival by means of petty crime, until as a young adult he went into criminal partnership with a man by the name of Compeyson, who had the advantages of a public-school education, a smooth manner, and good looks. Magwitch did Compeyson's dirty work for a long time, and they succeeded in a variety of scams, including a "bad thing with a rich woman" that netted them a handsome sum. Eventually they were both captured and tried for forgery, but Compeyson drew upon his gentlemanly manner, put most of the blame on the rough-hewn Magwitch, and got off with only half of Magwitch's punishment. Since then until the time he was banished, Magwitch explains, he had devoted himself to taking revenge on his former partner. Compeyson, it turns out, was the other convict whom Pip had seen on the marshes—the one with whom Magwitch was fighting so bitterly when he was captured. As Herbert listens to Magwitch's story, he puts two and two together, and hands Pip a note saying that Compeyson was the man who professed to be Miss Havisham's lover, jilted her, and swindled her out of a great deal of her family's money.

Pip's next step after hearing Magwitch's story is to go to Miss Havisham's and tell her that he now at last knows the identity of his patron (**chapter forty-four**). He tells her that this patron can not truly enrich him, and he requests that she take over subsidizing Herbert Pocket's career. Miss Havisham agrees only to consider supporting Herbert. She does admit that she intentionally mislead Pip into believing she was his benefactor, but she takes no responsibility for the unkindness of this behavior. Nor does Estella betray any regret when she tells Pip in spite of his final passionate declaration of love that she intends to marry Bentley Drummle. The only suggestion of any feeling on her part comes in the perverse form of her insistence that Pip can not really desire the love of one such as she who has no love to give. "Why," she asks, "should I fling myself upon the man who would soonest feel that I brought nothing to him?" As he leaves, Pip catches an unfamiliar look of "ghastly pity and remorse" on Miss Havisham's face.

Pip is prevented from returning to his flat after walking home from Miss Havisham's by a note from Wemmick in his mailbox saying only "Don't go home" (**chapter forty-five**). He rents a room for the night, spends the next day with Wemmick, who "in his private and personal capacity" tells Pip that he knows about his tenant, that this tenant is being watched, and that Compeyson is at large in London. Herbert has in the meantime taken Magwitch to a hidden apartment near the river, and Pip and he make plans to get Magwitch onto a steamer leaving the country at the nearest opportunity. Some weeks pass by anxiously but uneventfully as Pip gets into the habit of rowing on the river in the hopes that his eventual flight with Magwitch will thus be less conspicuous.

Preparations for escape are nearly complete when Jaggers approaches Pip to inform him that Miss Havisham would like to see him. Pip dines with Jaggers the evening before departing, and begins to pin down a resemblance which he had noticed before but had been unable to identify. Jaggers makes a point during dinner of showing off the extraordinarily strong hands of his maid, Molly. As Pip looks at her he realizes that she bears an uncanny resemblance to Estella (**chapter forty-eight**). "Her hands," he realizes, "were Estella's hands, and her eyes were

Estella's eyes." By the time he leaves he is convinced that Molly must somehow be Estella's mother. And on the way home he manages to persuade Wemmick to tell him Molly's story. Twenty years ago, it turns out, Molly was tried for murdering her own three-year-old child, as well as a woman ten years older and much larger and stronger. The crimes were committed, it was alleged, out of jealousy on her part over a "tramping man" to whom she was married and who was the father of her child. She was ultimately acquitted, Wemmick explains, due to brilliant defense work by Jaggers, who argued that she was physically incapable of strangling the stronger woman. He never dwelt on the strength of her hands then, Wemmick points out, but he does now.

Pip has a chance to follow up on his hunch the next day at Miss Havisham's (**chapter forty-nine**). To his great surprise, he finds Miss Havisham filled with regret and sorrow about her treatment of him and Estella. "What have I done! What have I done!" she cries repeatedly, wringing her hands and begging his forgiveness. She gives him nine hundred pounds to support Herbert, and when he asks her questions she tells him the truth. She does not know, she tells Pip, who Estella's mother is; Jaggers brought Estella to her about twenty years ago when she requested a child to play with. Pip sets out to leave, but halfway through the courtyard he is troubled by a vision of Miss Havisham hanging from a beam of the rotten old house. He returns inside to check on her, and finds her plunging toward him, "with a whirl of fire blazing all about her." Pip smothers the fire with the great cloth of the table that for so many years had been set in preparation for Miss Havisham's wedding.

The final piece in the puzzle of Estella's identity is provided by Herbert the next day as he dresses Pip's burnt hands (**chapter fifty**). Magwitch's mood has grown softer, Herbert tells Pip, and he has told him more of his story. It seems that when he was younger he was involved with a highly jealous and vengeful young woman. She was accused of murdering another woman by throttling her, but Jaggers defended her brilliantly, and she was acquitted. This woman and Magwitch had a child, but on the same night when the other woman was murdered she swore to Magwitch that she was going to destroy the child. Magwitch believes that this was done, although he does not know for sure, since he kept himself away from this time forward in order to avoid having to testify against her. Pip is certain by the time that Herbert finishes speaking that Magwitch is Estella's father.

This intuition is confirmed in Pip's subsequent interview with Jaggers in **chapter fifty-one**. Pip puts Jaggers at a disadvantage for the first time in their acquaintance by telling him that Magwitch is Estella's father. His hand thus forced, Jaggers discloses to Pip in characteristically guarded legal fashion the entire history of his relationship to Magwitch, Molly, and the young Estella. The tiny girl, he tells Pip, was placed in his trust by Molly at the same time that he was commissioned to find a girl companion for Miss Havisham. He struck a deal with Molly that if she really wished to save her daughter, she must be willing to give her up. In order to save the child from the fate of most of the orphans he encountered, he allowed the fiction that the child had been killed to continue circulating, and gave her to Miss Havisham. He concludes by insisting that Pip keep all this information in the strictest confidence, and objects violently when Pip salutes his kindess. "I'll have no feelings here," he insists, "get out."

In the concluding sequences of the novel (**chapters fifty-two through fifty-nine**), Pip narrowly escapes being slaughtered by Orlick, who confesses to his long resentment of Pip and to having killed Mrs. Joe. Magwitch, sadly, is not so lucky. His escape via the Thames is foiled, and he dies in a prison infirmary, but not before Pip has a chance to tell him that his daughter is alive and beautiful and that he is in love with her. After Magwitch's death, Pip passes into a delirious exhausted illness for several days. When he awakens he finds himself under the gentle care of Joe, who has paid his debts. He is to a great extent reconciled to Joe, and soon has the great satisfaction of attending Joe's wedding to Biddy. He goes to work for Herbert's company, and lives frugally as a bachelor with Herbert and Clara. He works hard, we are told, does well, and becomes the proud sponsor of little Pip—the child of Joe and Biddy. He also has one last encounter with Estella, who tells him of the unhappiness of her life with Bentley Drummle, and of their separation. In the original version of the novel their meeting is merely warm and cordial, and Pip sees that Estella's difficult experiences have made her a wiser person. In a revised version, Dickens implies that they are permanently reunited. ✤

—Neal Dolan
Harvard University

List of Characters

Pip (Philip Pirrip) is the hero and narrating voice of *Great Expectations*. An orphan left in the care of a shrewish older sister and her blacksmith husband, he aspires to become "a gentleman" in order to win the heart of a haughty girl, Estella, with whom he falls in love. Money from an anonymous benefactor allows him to move away from the rural village in which he grew up to the city of London, where he sets himself up as a gentleman. Surprising turns of events and unexpected connections between the people he meets teach him about the nature of his society and about the permanent value of his childhood loyalties.

Joe Gargery is, as Pip describes him, "a mild, good-natured, sweet-tempered, easy-going, foolish, dear fellow—a sort of Hercules in strength, and also in weakness." A blacksmith, he is married to Pip's older sister, and is both Pip's guardian and close companion early in the novel. He and Pip enjoy a variety of droll "larks," and Joe attempts to shield Pip from abusive treatment by his older sister. Pip's genteel aspirations and affectations later strain their intimacy, but Joe remains loyal to Pip, and comes to his aid when he finds himself in trouble. Joe embodies the virtues of the English working class as Dickens understood them, and stands at the sentimental heart of the novel.

Mrs. Joe is Pip's older sister and surrogate mother. Resentful that she must raise Pip "by hand" and that her husband is merely a blacksmith, she physically and verbally abuses both of them. She eventually dies as a result of a hammer blow to her head. The identity of her assailant is one of several mysteries which drive the plot.

Biddy, a wise and kindly relative of Mr. Wopsle, helps to educate Pip and becomes his confidante. She teaches him reading and writing, as well as some important lessons in basic human decency. After Mrs. Joe's death, she marries Joe, and they have a child who is named after Pip.

Abel Magwitch (Provis) is an escaped convict who is also Pip's anonymous benefactor, Estella's unknown father, one of

Jaggers's clients, and the former lover of Jaggers's maid Molly. Pip snitches food and a file for him at the beginning of the novel, thus earning his lifelong gratitude and support. From his exile in Australia, he secretly sends the money which enables Pip to educate himself and to become a gentleman. He is captured and dies in prison after returning to England toward the end of the novel.

Miss Havisham is an extremely wealthy and eccentric old lady who has secluded herself in her house for twenty years, since the day her would-be husband failed to show up for their wedding. She still dresses in her wedding outfit, refuses to move anything from the place it occupied on her wedding day, and has stopped all the clocks. Her only interest in life is to train her young charge, Estella, to take revenge on the male sex. Pip finally makes her see that she has deprived Estella of her humanity, and she begs Pip's forgiveness and immolates herself out of remorse.

Estella is a very pretty, haughty, and cold-hearted girl with whom Pip falls hopelessly in love upon first seeing her at Miss Havisham's house. She is raised by Miss Havisham to take revenge on all men, and she performs this role effectively in her treatment of Pip. She eventually marries a wealthy lout for his money, and suffers an unhappy marriage and a separation. Unbeknownst to her she is the daughter of the convict Magwitch and Jaggers's maid, Molly.

Herbert Pocket, upon first meeting Pip in the courtyard of Miss Havisham's house, says to him, "Let's fight." Pip proceeds to knock him down several times, but when they meet again years later in London they become the closest of friends. They take rooms together, and Herbert draws tactfully on his genteel upbringing to help Pip smooth out some of his rough edges. Pip uses his fortune to help Herbert get started in business, and eventually goes to work in the same firm. At the close of the novel we are told that Pip goes to live with Herbert and his wife.

Jaggers is a brilliant and domineering lawyer who provides the link between the various social levels depicted in the novel. He administers the financial affairs of both Miss Havisham and

Magwitch, and becomes Pip's legal sponsor. He functions as a symbol of urban professionalism at its best and worst extremes. He is efficient, punctual, articulate, and dynamic; but he is also impersonal, cold, arrogant, and obsessed with control.

Wemmick is Jaggers's assistant. Like Jaggers, Wemmick is grimly professional in his capacity as an agent of the law. His motto is "get sortable property" (i.e., money). But Pip finds that behind the walls of a home that is literally his castle, he is spontaneous, kind, and playful. He takes tender care of his aging father, and goes to great lengths to help Pip and Herbert Pocket.

Bentley Drummle is an aristocratic rival of Pip's for the attentions of Estella. He is described as unintelligent, selfish, deceitful, and proud. His family riches nonetheless win him Estella's hand in marriage.

Orlick is a violent, resentful, and dangerous journeyman blacksmith. He bludgeons Mrs. Joe with a hammer early in the novel, and in the closing moments he very nearly kills Pip.

Pumblechook is an alternately pompous and obsequious cornchandler who is a friend of Mrs. Joe. He lectures Pip about the natural viciousness of children until Pip comes into money, at which point he fawns upon him shamelessly.

Compeyson is the second convict who Pip sees on the marshes at the beginning of the novel. His sophisticated upbringing allowed him to take terrible advantage of Magwitch when they were partners in crime, and Magwitch is thus determined to take revenge upon him at all costs. He is also the man who left Miss Havisham standing at the altar, and made off with a good deal of her money. ❖

Critical Views

[Edwin P. Whipple (1819–1886) was one of the leading
American literary critics and reviewers of the nine-
teenth century. Among his many books are *Essays and
Reviews* (1848) and *The Literature of the Age of
Elizabeth* (1869). In this review of *Great Expectations,*
Whipple studies the novel in relation to other works by
Dickens, suggesting that it represents a transition from
his earlier, purely comic works to works of a more seri-
ous cast.]

In *Great Expectations* ⟨. . .⟩ Dickens seems to have attained the
mastery of powers which formerly more or less mastered him.
He has fairly discovered that he cannot, like Thackeray, narrate
a story as if he were a mere looker-on, a mere 'knowing'
observer of what he describes and represents; and he has
therefore taken observation simply as the basis of his plot and
his characterization. As we read *Vanity Fair* and *The New-
comes,* we are impressed with the actuality of the persons and
incidents. There is an absence both of directing ideas and dis-
turbing idealizations. Everything drifts to its end, as in real life.
In *Great Expectations* there is shown a power of external observation finer and deeper even than Thackeray's; and yet, owing
to the presence of other qualities, the general impression is not
one of objective reality. The author palpably uses his observations as materials for his creative faculties to work upon; he
does not record, but invents; and he produces something
which is natural only under conditions prescribed by his own
mind. He shapes, disposes, penetrates, colors, and contrives
everything, and the whole action is a series of events which
could have occurred only in his own brain, and which it is difficult to conceive of as actually 'happening.' And yet in none of
his other works does he evince a shrewder insight into real life,
and a clearer perception and knowledge of what is called 'the
world.' The book is, indeed, an artistic creation, and not a mere
succession of humorous and pathetic scenes, and demonstrates

that Dickens is now in the prime, and not in the decline of his great powers.

The characters of the novel also show how deeply it has been meditated; for, though none of them may excite the personal interest which clings to Sam Weller or little Dombey, they are better fitted to each other and to the story in which they appear than is usual with Dickens. They all combine to produce that unity of impression which the work leaves on the mind. Individually they will rank among the most original of the author's creations. ⟨. . .⟩

The style of the romance is rigorously close to things. The author is so engrossed with the objects before his mind, is so thoroughly in earnest, that he has fewer of those humorous caprices of expression in which formerly he was wont to wanton. Some of the old hilarity and play of fancy is gone, but we hardly miss it in our admiration of the effects produced by his almost stern devotion to the main idea of his work. There are passages of description and narrative in which we are hardly conscious of the words, in our clear apprehension of the objects and incidents they convey. The quotable epithets and phrases are less numerous than in *Dombey and Son* and *David Copperfield;* but the scenes and events impressed on the imagination are perhaps greater in number and more vivid in representation. The poetical element of the writer's genius, his modification of the forms, hues, and sounds of Nature by viewing them through the medium of an imagined mind, is especially prominent throughout the descriptions with which the work abounds. Nature is not only described, but individualized and humanized.

Altogether we take great joy in recording our conviction that *Great Expectations* is a masterpiece. We have never sympathized in the mean delight which some critics seem to experience in detecting the signs which subtly indicate the decay of power in creative intellects. We sympathize still less in the stupid and ungenerous judgments of those who find a still meaner delight in wilfully asserting that the last book of a popular writer is unworthy of the genius which produced his first. In our opinion, *Great Expectations* is a work which proves that we may expect from Dickens a series of romances far exceeding in power and artistic skill the productions which have already given him such a preëminence among the novelists of the age.

—Edwin P. Whipple, [Review of *Great Expectations*], *Atlantic Monthly* 8, No. 3 (September 1861): 380–82

❖

MARGARET OLIPHANT ON *GREAT EXPECTATIONS* AS A SENSATIONAL NOVEL

[Margaret Oliphant (1828–1897) was a prolific Scottish novelist and essayist. Among her critical works is the noted *Literary History of England* (1882). In this joint review of *Great Expectations* and Wilkie Collins's *The Woman in White* (1860), Oliphant praises Dickens's characters but believes Collins's novel to be a better example of the "sensational novel," or the novel of stirring and vivid incidents.]

The secondary persons of this book ⟨. . .⟩—almost entirely separated as they are from the main action, which is connected only in the very slightest way with the rest of the story—are, so far as they possess any individual character at all, specimens of oddity run mad. The incredible ghost, in the wedding-dress which has lasted for five-and-twenty years, is scarcely more *outré* than the ridiculous Mrs Pocket. ⟨. . .⟩ Of the same description is the ingenious Mr Wemmick, the lawyer's clerk, who lives in a little castle at Walworth, and calls his old father the Aged, and exclaims, "Hulloa! here's a church—let's go in!' when he is going to be married. Is this fun? Mr Dickens ought to be an authority in that respect, seeing he has made more honest laughter in his day than any man living, and called forth as many honest tears; but we confess it looks exceedingly dull pleasantry to us, and that we are slow to accept Mr Wemmick's carpentry as a substitute for all the homely wit and wisdom in which Mr Dickens's privileged humorists used to abound. Besides all this heavy sport, there is a sensation episode of a still heavier description, for the introduction of which we are totally unable to discover any motive, except that of filling a few additional pages—unless, perhaps, it might be a desperate expedient on the part of the author to rouse his own languid interest in the conduct of the piece. Otherwise, why Pip should be seduced into the clutches of the senseless brute Orlick, and made to endure all the agonies of death for nothing, is a mystery quite beyond our powers of guessing. And again Mr Dickens misses fire—he rouses himself up, indeed, and bethinks himself of his old arts of word and composition, and does his best to galvanise his figures into momentary life. But it is plain to see all along that he means nothing by it; we are as sure that help will come at the right moment, as if we saw it approaching all the time; and the whole affair is the most arbitrary and causeless stoppage in the story—perhaps acceptable to weekly readers, as a prick of meretricious excitement on the languid road, perhaps a little stimulant to the mind of the writer, who was bored with his own production— but as a part of a narrative totally uncalled for, an interruption and encumbrance, interfering with the legitimate interest of the story, which is never so strong as to bear much trifling with. In every way, Mr Dickens's performance must yield precedence to the companion work of his disciple and assistant. The elder writer, rich in genius and natural power, has, from indolence or caprice, or the confidence of established popularity, produced, with all his unquestionable advantages, and with a subject admirably qualified to afford the most striking and picturesque effects, a very ineffective and colourless work; the younger, with no such gifts, has employed the common action of life so as to call forth the most original and startling impressions upon the mind of the reader. The lesson to be read therefrom is one so profoundly improving that it might form the moral of any Good-child story. Mr Dickens is the careless, clever boy who could do it twice as well, but won't take pains. Mr Wilkie Collins is the steady fellow, who pegs at his lesson like a hero, and wins the prize over the other's head. Let the big children and the little perpend and profit by the lesson. The most popular of writers would do well to pause before he yawns and flings his careless essay at the public, and to consider that the reputation which makes everything he produces externally suc-

cessful is itself mortal, and requires a sustenance more substantial than a languid owner can be expected to give.
 —Margaret Oliphant, "Sensational Novels," *Blackwood's Edinburgh Magazine* No. 559 (May 1862): 579–80

❖

JOHN FORSTER ON THE WRITING OF *GREAT EXPECTATIONS*

[John Forster (1812–1876) was a distinguished British critic and biographer who wrote biographies of Oliver Goldsmith (1848), Walter Savage Landor (1869), and other writers. In this extract, taken from his landmark biography of Dickens (1872–74), Forster draws upon primary documents—especially letters by Dickens—to reveal Dickens's state of mind as he wrote *Great Expectations.*]

A Tale of Two Cities was published in 1859; the series of papers collected as the *Uncommercial Traveller* were occupying Dickens in 1860; and it was while engaged in these, and throwing off in the course of them capital "samples" of fun and enjoyment, he thus replied to a suggestion that he should let himself loose upon some single humorous conception, in the vein of his youthful achievements in that way. "For a little piece I have been writing—or am writing; for I hope to finish it to-day—such a very fine new, and grotesque idea has opened upon me, that I begin to doubt whether I had not better cancel the little paper, and reserve the notion for a new book. You shall judge as soon as I get it printed. But it so opens out before *me* that I can see the whole of a serial revolving on it, in a most singular and comic manner." This was the germ of Pip and Magwitch, which at first he intended to make the ground work of a tale in the old twenty-number form, but for reasons perhaps fortunate brought afterwards within the limits of a less elaborate novel. "Last week," he wrote on the 4th of October, 1860, "I got to work on the new story. I had previously very carefully considered the state and prospects of *All the Year*

Round, and, the more I considered them, the less hope I saw of being able to get back, *now,* to the profit of a separate publication in the old 20 numbers." (A tale, which at the time was appearing in his serial, had disappointed expectation.)

"However, I worked on, knowing that what I was doing would run into another groove; and I called a council of war at the office on Tuesday. It was perfectly clear that the one thing to be done was, for me to strike in. I have therefore decided to begin the story as of the length of the *Tale of Two Cities* on the first of December—begin publishing, that is. I must make the most I can out of the book. You shall have the first two or three weekly parts to-morrow. The name is GREAT EXPECTATIONS. I think a good name?" Two days later he wrote: "The sacrifice of *Great Expectations* is really and truly made for myself. The property of *All the Year Round* is far too valuable, in every way, to be much endangered. Our fall is not large, but we have a considerable advance in hand of the story we are now publishing, and there is no vitality in it, and no chance whatever of stopping the fall; which on the contrary would be certain to increase. Now, if I went into a twenty-number serial, I should cut off my power of doing anything serial here for two good years—and that would be a most perilous thing. On the other hand, by dashing in now, I come in when most wanted; and if Reade and Wilkie follow me, our course, will be shaped out handsomely and hopefully for between two and three years. A thousand pounds are to be paid for early proofs of the story to America." A few more days brought the first instalment of the tale, and explanatory mention of it. "The book will be written in the first person throughout, and during these first three weekly numbers you will find the hero to be a boy-child, like David. Then he will be an apprentice. You will not have to complain of the want of humour as in the *Tale of Two Cities.* I have made the opening, I hope, in its general effect exceedingly droll. I have put a child and a good-natured foolish man, in relations that seem to me very funny. Of course I have got in the pivot on which the story will turn too—and which indeed, as you remember, was the grotesque tragi-comic conception that first encouraged me. To be quite sure I had fallen into no unconscious repetitions, I read *David Copperfield* again the other

day, and was affected by it to a degree you would hardly
believe."

—John Forster, *The Life of Charles Dickens* (London: Chatto &
Windus, 1872–74), Vol. 3, pp. 327–29

❖

G. K. CHESTERTON ON THE CHARACTERS IN *GREAT EXPECTATIONS*

[G. K. Chesterton (1874–1936), although today best
known as the author of the Father Brown detective stories, was a prolific writer on literature, religion, philoso-
phy, and society. He had a particular affinity for
Dickens, writing introductions to many of Dickens's
novels as well as a critical study, *Charles Dickens*
(1906). In this extract, Chesterton maintains that, in
spite of Dickens's attempt to write a serious, realistic
novel, *Great Expectations* nevertheless contains those
larger-than-life characters that distinguish Dickens's
entire work.]

We might very well, as I have remarked elsewhere, apply to all
Dickens's books the title *Great Expectations*. All his books are
full of an airy and yet ardent expectation of everything; of the
next person who shall happen to speak, of the next chimney
that shall happen to smoke, of the next event, of the next
ecstasy; of the next fulfilment of any eager human fancy. All his
books might be called *Great Expectations*. But the only book to
which he gave the name of *Great Expectations* was the only
book in which the expectation was never realised. It was so
with the whole of that splendid and unconscious generation to
which he belonged. The whole glory of that old English middle
class was that it was unconscious; its excellence was entirely in
that, that it was the culture of the nation, and that it did not
know it. If Dickens had ever known that he was optimistic, he
would have ceased to be happy.

It is necessary to make this first point clear: that in *Great
Expectations* Dickens was really trying to be a quiet, a

detached, and even a cynical observer of human life. Dickens was trying to be Thackeray. And the final and startling triumph of Dickens is this: that even to this moderate and modern story, he gives an incomparable energy which is not moderate and which is not modern. He is trying to be reasonable; but in spite of himself he is inspired. He is trying to be detailed, but in spite of himself he is gigantic. Compared to the rest of Dickens this is Thackeray; but compared to the whole of Thackeray we can only say in supreme praise of it that it is Dickens.

Take, for example, the one question of snobbishness. Dickens has achieved admirably the description of the doubts and vanities of the wretched Pip as he walks down the street in his new gentlemanly clothes, the clothes of which he is so proud and so ashamed. Nothing could be so exquisitely human, nothing especially could be so exquisitely masculine as that combination of self-love and self-assertion and even insolence with a naked and helpless sensibility to the slightest breath of ridicule. Pip thinks himself better than every one else, and yet anybody can snub him; that is the everlasting male, and perhaps the everlasting gentleman. Dickens has described perfectly this quivering and defenceless dignity. Dickens has described perfectly how ill-armed it is against the coarse humour of real humanity—the real humanity which Dickens loved, but which idealists and philanthropists do not love, the humanity of cabmen and costermongers and men singing in a third-class carriage; the humanity of Trabb's boy. In describing Pip's weakness Dickens is as true and as delicate as Thackeray. But Thackeray might have been easily as true and as delicate as Dickens. This quick and quiet eye for the tremors of mankind is a thing which Dickens possessed, but which others possessed also. ⟨. . .⟩ The thing about any figure of Dickens, about Sam Weller or Dick Swiveller, or Micawber, or Bagstock, or Trabb's boy,—the thing about each one of these persons is that he cannot be exhausted. A Dickens character hits you first on the nose and then in the waistcoat, and then in the eye and then in the waistcoat again, with the blinding rapidity of some battering engine. The scene in which Trabb's boy continually overtakes Pip in order to reel and stagger as at a first encounter is a thing quite within the real competence of such a character; it might have been suggested by Thackeray, or George Eliot, or any realist. But the point with Dickens is that there is a rush in the boy's rushings; the writer and the reader rush with him. They start with him, they stare with him, they stagger with him, they share an inexpressible vitality in the air which emanates from this violent and capering satirist. Trabb's boy is among other things a boy; he has a physical rapture in hurling himself like a boomerang and in bouncing to the sky like a ball. It is just exactly in describing this quality that Dickens is Dickens and that no one else comes near him.

> —G. K. Chesterton, *Criticisms and Appreciations of the Works of Charles Dickens* (London: J. M. Dent; New York: E. P. Dutton [Everyman's Library], 1911), pp. 200–203

❖

GEORGE BERNARD SHAW ON THE WOMEN IN *GREAT EXPECTATIONS*

[George Bernard Shaw (1856–1950) was perhaps the leading British playwright of his time, but he also wrote a number of critical essays. In this extract, Shaw focuses on the women in *Great Expectations,* claiming rather tartly that personal difficulties in Dickens's life colored his portrayal of Estella and other figures.]

Estella is a curious addition to the gallery of unamiable women painted by Dickens. In my youth it was commonly said that Dickens could not draw women. The people who said this were thinking of Agnes Wickfield and Esther Summerson, of Little Dorrit and Florence Dombey, and thinking of them as ridiculous idealizations of their sex. Gissing put a stop to that by asking whether shrews like Mrs. Raddle, Mrs. Macstinger, Mrs. Gargery, fools like Mrs. Nickleby and Flora Finching, warped spinsters like Rosa Dartle and Miss Wade, were not masterpieces of woman drawing. And they are all unamiable. But for Betsy Trotwood, who is a very lovable fairy godmother and yet a genuine nature study, and an old dear like Mrs. Boffin, one would be tempted to ask whether Dickens had ever in his life met an amiable female. The transformation of Dora into Flora is diabolical, but frightfully true to nature. Of course Dickens with his imagination could invent amiable women by the dozen; but somehow he could not or would not bring them to life as he brought the others. We doubt whether he ever knew a little Dorrit; but Fanny Dorrit is from the life unmistakably. So is Estella. She is a much more elaborate study than Fanny, and, I should guess, a recent one.

Dickens, when he let himself go in *Great Expectations,* was separated from his wife and free to make more intimate acquaintances with women than a domesticated man can. I know nothing of his adventures in this phase of his career, though I daresay a good deal of it will be dug out by the little sect of anti-Dickensites whose fanaticism has been provoked by the Dickens Fellowships. It is not necessary to suggest a love affair; for Dickens could get from a passing glance a hint which he could expand into a full-grown character. The point concerns us here only because it is the point on which the ending of *Great Expectations* turns: namely, that Estella is a born tormentor. She deliberately torments Pip all through for the fun of it; and in the little we hear of her intercourse with others there is no suggestion of a moment of kindness: in fact her tormenting of Pip is almost affectionate in contrast to the cold disdain of her attitude towards the people who were not worth tormenting. It is not surprising that the unfortunate Bentley Drummle, whom she marries in the stupidity of sheer perversity, is obliged to defend himself from her clever malice with his fists: a consolation to us for Pip's broken heart, but not altogether a credible one; for the real Estellas can usually intimidate the real Bentley Drummles. At all events the final sugary suggestion of Estella redeemed by Bentley's thrashings and waste of her money, and living happily with Pip for ever after, provoked even Dickens's eldest son to rebel against it, most justly.

—George Bernard Shaw, "Foreword" to *Great Expectations* (1937; rev. 1947), *Shaw on Dickens,* ed. Dan H. Laurence and Martin Quinn (New York: Ungar, 1985), pp. 56–57

❖

[John H. Hagan, Jr. is a literary scholar and author of several articles on English literature. In this extract, Hagan believes social injustice to be the central issue in *Great Expectations*.]

Injustice is thus at the heart of the matter—injustice working upon and through the elders of Pip and Estella, and continuing its reign in the children themselves. With these children, therefore, we have a theme analogous to one deeply pondered by another great Victorian novelist: the idea of "consequences" as developed by George Eliot. Both she and Dickens are moved by a terrifying vision of the wide extent to which pollution can penetrate the different, apparently separate and unrelated, members of society. Once an act of injustice has been committed, there is no predicting to what extent it will affect the lives of generations yet unborn and of people far removed in the social scale from the victims of the original oppression. Though on a smaller scale, Dickens succeeds no less in *Great Expectations* than in his larger panoramic novels in suggesting a comprehensive social situation. No less than in *Bleak House, Little Dorrit,* and *Our Mutual Friend*—and in *A Tale of Two Cities* as well—the different levels of society are brought together in a web of sin, injustice, crime, and destruction. The scheme bears an analogy to the hereditary diseases running throughout several generations in Zola's *Les Rougons-Macquarts* series. Dickens compresses his material more than Zola by starting *in medias res,* and showing Pip as the focal point for the past, present, and future at once. In him are concentrated the effects of previous injustice, and he holds in himself the injustice yet to come. The interest of the novel is never restricted merely to the present. Dickens opens a great vista, a "poor labyrinth," through which we may see the present as but the culmination of a long history of social evil. Society is never able to smother wholly the facts of its injustice. As Dickens shows in novel after novel, somehow these facts will come to light again: Bounderby's mother in *Hard Times* rises to reveal her son's hypocrisy to the crowd he has bullied for so many years; the facts of Mrs. Clennam's relationship to the Dorrit family, and of society's injury to Lady Dedlock, her lover, and her child, are all unearthed in the end. Immediate victims may be skillfully suppressed, as Magwitch, returning from exile, is finally caught and imprisoned again. But the baleful effects of social evil go on in a kind of incalculable chain reaction. It is the old theme of tragic drama read into the bleak world of Mid-Victorian England: the sins of the fathers will be visited upon the heads of their children; the curse on the house will have to be expiated by future generations of sufferers.

Thus it is fair to say that Pip's story is more than a study of personal development. In his lonely struggle to work out his salvation, he is atoning for the guilt of society at large. In learning to rise above selfishness, to attain to a selfless love for Magwitch, he brings to an end the chain of evil that was first forged by the selfish Compeyson. His regeneration has something of the same force as Krook's "spontaneous combustion" in *Bleak House,* or the collapse of the Clennam mansion in *Little Dorrit,* or even the renunciation of his family heritage by Charles Darnay in *A Tale of Two Cities.* Just as Darnay must atone for the guilt of his family by renouncing his property, so Pip must atone for the evils of the society that has corrupted him by relinquishing his unearned wealth. And as Darnay marries the girl whose father was one of the victims of his family's oppression, so Pip desires to marry the girl whose father, Magwitch, is the victim of the very society whose values Pip himself has embraced.

—John H. Hagan, Jr., "The Poor Labyrinth: The Theme of Social Injustice in Dickens's *Great Expectations," Nineteenth-Century Fiction* 9, No. 3 (November 1954): 173–74

❖

J. HILLIS MILLER ON THE ENDING OF *GREAT EXPECTATIONS*

[J. Hillis Miller (b. 1928) is one of the leading literary critics and theorists of our time and the author of many books, including *The Disappearance of God* (1958), *The Form of Victorian Fiction* (1968), and *The Ethics of Reading* (1987). After teaching at Johns Hopkins and

Yale, he is now a professor of English at the University of California at Irvine. In this extract, Miller defends the ending of *Great Expectations,* in which Dickens, at the advice of his friend, the novelist Edward Bulwer-Lytton, caused Pip and Estella to be reconciled. Most critics have condemned this ending as being contrived, but Miller sees it as consistent with a religious analogue, the expulsion from Eden.]

The divine power functions in *Great Expectations* primarily as the supreme judge before whom all social distinctions are as nothing: "The sun was striking in at the great windows of the court, through the glittering drops of rain upon the glass, and it made a broad shaft of light between the two-and-thirty [criminals] and the Judge, linking both together, and perhaps reminding some among the audience, how both were passing on, with absolute equality, to the greater Judgment that knoweth all things and cannot err." There is a true religious motif here. The light is God's judgment before which earthly judge and earthly judged, gentleman and common thief, are equal. But the meaning of the passage is as much social as religious. It is a final dramatization of the fact that social eminence such as Pip had sought and social judgments such as have hounded Magwitch all his life are altogether unimportant as sources of selfhood. At the center of Dickens' novels is a recognition of the bankruptcy of the relation of the individual to society as it now exists, the objective structure of given institutions and values. Only what an individual makes of himself, in charitable relations to others, counts. And this self-creation tends to require open revolt against the pressures of society. Human beings are themselves the source of the transcendence of their isolation.

Once Pip has established his new relationship to Magwitch he is able at last to win Estella. Pip's final love for Estella is a single complex relation which is both identification with the loved person (he is no longer conscious of a lack, a void of unfulfilled desire), and separation (he is still aware of himself as a self, as a separate identity; he does not melt into the loved person, and lose himself altogether). As in *Little Dorrit* and *A Tale of Two Cities,* the irreducible otherness, the permanent area of mystery in the loved one, is recognized and maintained.

Pip and Estella have experienced before their union their most complete separation, Pip in the agony of his discovery that Estella is not destined for him and that Magwitch is his real benefactor, and Estella in her unhappy marriage to Bentley Drummle, who has "used her with great cruelty," just as Pip has been "used" by Estella. These experiences have transformed them both. It is only when Estella has been tamed by the cruelty of her bad husband that she and Pip can enter into a wholly different relationship. Only when Estella's proud, cold glance is transformed into "the saddened softened light of the once proud eyes" can she and Pip transform the fettering of slave by master into the handclasp of love. Estella too must suffer the slave's loss of selfhood in order to be herself transformed. Both have come back from a kind of death to meet and join in the moonlight in Miss Havisham's ruined garden. The second ending is, in my opinion, the best. Not only was it, after all, the one Dickens published (would he really have acceded to Mrs. Grundy in the mask of Bulwer-Lytton without reasons of his own?), but, it seems to me, the second ending, in joining Pip and Estella, is much truer to the real direction of the story. The paragraphs which, in the second version of the ending, close the novel remind us, in their echo of Milton, that Estella and Pip are accepting their exile from the garden of false hopes. Now that the mists of infatuation have cleared away Pip and Estella are different persons. They go forth from the ruined garden into a fallen world. In this world their lives will be given meaning only by their own acts and by their dependence on one another. Pip now has all that he wanted, Estella and her jewels, but what he has is altogether different from what he expected. Rather than possessing the impossible reconciliation of freedom and security he had sought in Estella and in gentility, he now loves and is loved by another fallible and imperfect being like himself:

> The silvery mist was touched with the first rays of the moonlight, and the same rays touched the tears that dropped from her eyes. . . .

I took her hand in mine, and we went out of the ruined place; and, as the morning mists had risen long ago when I first left the forge, so, the evening mists were rising now, and in all the broad expanse of tranquil light they showed to me, I saw no shadow of another parting from her.

—J. Hillis Miller, *Charles Dickens: The World of His Novels* (Cambridge, MA: Harvard University Press, 1958), pp. 276–78

❖

Monroe Engel on the Evil of Property

[Monroe Engel (b. 1921), a former professor of English at Harvard University, is a novelist as well as the author of *The Maturity of Dickens* (1959), from which the following extract is taken. Here, Engel identifies the central focus of *Great Expectations* as a rumination on the evil of property.]

The evil of property lies in its tendency to use its possessors instead of being used by them. The point is made unambiguously and with force. Pip's first genuine act in *Great Expectations,* and an act from which ensue the consequences that in good part make the novel, is to steal food and a file from his home for the starving escaped convict Magwitch. It is notable that the guilt that haunts his mind has nothing to do with the genuinely serious matter of aiding an escaped and dangerous convict. It is his own theft he worries about, and not so much the stolen file as the stolen food, the broken vittles. Joe Gargery, who remains in the Eden of innocence throughout the novel, and is the control or fixed point in relation to which Pip's wandering is measured, makes overt the moral significance of this theft, when the escaped convict, to protect Pip, says that it was he who stole the food from the Gargerys' house: " 'God knows you're welcome to it—so far as it was ever mine,' returned Joe, with a saving remembrance of Mrs. Joe. 'We don't know what you have done, but we wouldn't have you starved to death for it, poor miserable fellow creature—Would us, Pip?' "

Joe tries to bolster Pip in his innocence, but Mrs. Joe is another matter. For her, property is sacred and uncomfortable, like some people's religion. Her preparations for Christmas dinner blight the holiday, and when she walks to town, she carries "a basket like the Great Seal of England in plaited straw, a pair of pattens, a spare shawl, and an umbrella, though it was a fine bright day." Pip was not clear whether "these articles were carried penitentially or ostentatiously," but he thought they were probably "displayed as articles of property—much as Cleopatra or any other soverign lady on the Rampage might exhibit her wealth in a pageant or procession."

Pumblechook (a good example of Dickens' genius for fitting names) is far worse than Mrs. Gargery, and it is he who pushes Pip into the Havisham connection, bullies and maltreats him, flatters him when his fortunes are risen, and turns on him self-righteously and full of injury when they fall. But the real nightmare of property is provided by Miss Havisham in Satis House. A rough irony of names is used frequently in *Great Expectations,* starting with the title itself; of the name of the Havisham house, Estella says: "I meant when it was given, that whoever had this house, could want nothing else. They must have been easily satisfied in those days, I should think." In a ruin of old symbolic goods, Miss Havisham lives a living death, and plots her vicarious vengeance on victims who have only a token culpability for her tragedy. It is her goods, her wealth, that have ruined her in the first place by attracting Compeyson to her, and now she will have the goods work in reverse, by making Estella rich, impregnable, heart-breaking.

—Monroe Engel, *The Maturity of Dickens* (Cambridge, MA: Harvard University Press, 1959), pp. 159–60

❖

SYLVÈRE MONOD ON THE MORALITY OF *GREAT EXPECTATIONS*

[Sylvère Monod (b. 1921), a former professor of English at the Sorbonne in Paris, is a leading scholar on Dickens. He has written *Dickens the Novelist* (1968) and a study, *Martin Chuzzlewit* (1985), and (with George Lord) has edited *Hard Times* (1966) and *Bleak House* (1977). In this extract, Monod finds the true significance of *Great Expectations* to lie in its moral outlook, particularly in its scorn of snobbery and the worship of money.]

⟨. . .⟩ much of the significance of *Great Expectations* to-day comes from the moral and social purport of the book. Here again, the extraordinary wealth of its implications and suggestions in those fields, will be best appreciated by each individual reader when he has discovered them for himself, when they have thus become part of his moral experience; and the force of those revelations and confirmations will be increased after each fresh contact with the book. I for one am warned by repeated past experience—and by experience in the very recent past—against regarding any of my own findings as final, or the list as closed. Besides, such discoveries are intensely personal matters, so that they can hardly be shared, least of all publicly. And the different findings of different readers need not be mutually exclusive; the moral truth in *Great Expectations* is manifold, and can be apprehended in any number of fragmentary ways. I can do no more therefore, than mention one of the most significant directions in which I at present think this truth is to be looked for. I tend to see in *Great Expectations,* in so far as social and moral criticism is at stake, above all a passionate denunciation of the false values on which the Victorian ideals of gentlemanliness rested: humbug—that lifelong bugbear of Dickens—smugness, and all the snobberies entailed by an exclusive regard for, or even worship of, money and its consequences in the form of rank, are all tirelessly and relentlessly exposed.

Now, this, if it were all, even expressed with exceptional vigour, the vigour of strong personal conviction, would be most unoriginal, and it would not justify the claim I am trying to make. Perhaps both Carlyle and Ruskin, among others, were preaching the same creed with greater moral elevation and greater efficacy. But I think this is not all. For indeed, thanks to the autobiographical form, Dickens can picture the groping quest of Pip for the truth, not only about the world and the society among which he lives, but also, and more importantly, about himself. Thus he will perceive his own deficiencies, and such perceptions will be as many steps in his spiritual progress. Sometimes he will not be aware of them, but will disclose them to us unwillingly, as it were, or at any rate unwittingly, and they will be all the more significant to us on that account.

Thus does Dickens make it abundantly clear that the worst and most insidious kind of smugness may lie in the complacent, Pharisaical, condemnation of other people's smugness. Pip, even while he lays bare the humbug of Pumblechook, or the sycophantic greed of Miss Havisham's relatives, or the snobbery of his comrade Drummle, is a pitiful little snob himself. The word *snob* is not used once by Dickens in *Great Expectations,* yet a considerable proportion of the book consists of infinite and subtle variations on this theme of snobbery. One thing is rather explicitly brought to light; it is that Pip will never be a man before he has ceased to wish to become merely a gentleman, before he has discarded all his spurious ambitions. This is already of the utmost significance, and it is beautifully conveyed. But I think the implications of Pip's moral adventure are much more far-reaching than that. And what makes the book so exceedingly valuable even to-day, a hundred years after, is perhaps above all the effect it must inevitably produce on us, the suggestion that it will never do to lay the whole blame on the Victorians; such a comfortable attitude would be a hindrance, not a help, on the way to truth and moral progress. *Great Expectations* invites us to turn our ruthless glance on to ourselves, and to see that there is smugness, that there is humbug, that there is Victorianism of a kind, that there is this yearning for pseudo-gentility and this unslakable thirst for money, not in the Victorians merely, but in man in general, in the men of all times, in the men of the present day, in us.

And then, in the same way as Pip emerges out of his ordeal with clearer perceptions, we can emerge out of the reading and re-reading of *Great Expectations* with a better understanding of some vital truths. *Great Expectations* is probably Dickens's most fully adult novel, staging as it does in Pip an adult in the making; why not let the book help make adults of all its readers? Then would the title of the novel, unquestionably far and away the richest, most beautiful, most pathetic of the whole fifteen coined by Dickens, assume an ever fresh significance. Pip's expectations were as deceptive as they were, not great, but contemptibly little; so were Miss Havisham's, or Magwitch's. But our own expectations on opening the book, for the first or the hundredth time, cannot be disappointed, whether we go to it for amusement, or for emotion, or for what alone can make expectations truly great: the truth.

—Sylvère Monod, "*Great Expectations* a Hundred Years After," *Dickensian* 56 (1960): 139–40

❖

JULIAN MOYNAHAN ON PIP AS DICKENS'S MOST COMPLEX HERO

[Julian Moynahan (b. 1925), a professor of English at Rutgers University, is a novelist and critic. He has written *Vladimir Nabokov* (1971), *Anglo-Irish: The Literary Imagination in a Hyphenated Culture* (1995), and other works. In this extract, Moynahan finds Pip to be Dickens's most complex hero in his combination of virtues and flaws.]

In this essay I have argued that Dickens's novel defines its hero's dream of great expectations and the consequences stemming from indulgence in that dream under the two aspects of desire and will, of regressive longing for an excess of love and of violent aggressiveness. In the unfolding of the action these two dramas are not presented separately. Instead they are combined into Dickens's most complex representation of character in action. Pip is Dickens's most complicated hero, demonstrating at once the traits of criminal and gull, of victimiser and victim. He is victimised by his dream and the dream itself, by virtue of its profoundly anti-social and unethical nature, forces him into relation with a world in which other human beings fall victim to his drive for power. He is, in short, a hero sinned against and sinning: sinned against because in the first place the dream was thrust upon the helpless child by powerful and corrupt figures from the adult world; a sinner because in accepting for himself a goal in life based upon unbridled individualism and indifference to others he takes up a career which *Great Expectations* repeatedly, through a variety of artistic means, portrays as essentially criminal.

After Magwitch's death, Pip falls a prey to brain fever. During his weeks of delirium it seems to me that his hallucinations articulate the division in his character between helpless passivity and demonic aggressiveness. Pip tells us he dreamed

> that I was a brick in the house wall, and yet entreating to be released from the giddy place where the builders had set me; that I was a steel beam of a vast engine clashing and whirling over a great gulf, yet that I implored in my own person to have the engine stopped, and my part in it hammered off.

It is tempting to read these images as dream logic. The hero-victim cries for release from his unsought position of height and power, but cannot help himself from functioning as a moving part of a monstrous apparatus which seems to sustain itself from a plunge into the abyss only through the continuous expenditure of destructive force. In the narrative's full context this vast engine can be taken to represent at one and the same time the demonic side of the hero's career and a society that maintains its power intact by the continuous destruction of the hopes and lives of its weaker members. In the latter connection we can think of Magwitch's account of his childhood and youth, and of the judge who passed a death sentence on thirty-two men and women, while the sun struck in through the courtroom windows making a 'broad shaft of light between the two-and-thirty and the judge, linking them both together'. But to think of the engine as a symbol of society is still to think of Pip. For Pip's career enacts his society's condition of being—its guilt, its sinfulness, and in the end, its helplessness to cleanse itself of a taint 'of prison and crime'.

When Pip wakes up from his delirium he finds himself a child again, safe in the arms of the angelic Joe Gargery. But the guilt of great expectations remains inexpiable, and the cruelly beautiful original ending of the novel remains the only possible 'true' ending. Estella and Pip face each other across the insurmountable barrier of lost innocence. The novel dramatises the loss of innocence, and does not glibly present the hope of a redemptory second birth for either its guilty hero or the guilty society which shaped him. I have already said that Pip's fantasy of superabundant love brings him at last to a point of alienation from the real world. And similarly Pip's fantasy of power brings him finally to a point where withdrawal is the only positive moral response left to him.

The brick is taken down from its giddy place, a part of the engine is hammered off. Pip cannot redeem his world. In no conceivable sense a leader, he can only lead himself into a sort of exile from his society's power centres. Living abroad as the partner of a small, unambitious firm, he is to devote his remaining life to doing the least possible harm to the smallest number of people, so earning a visitor's privileges in the lost paradise where Biddy and Joe, the genuine innocents of the novel, flourish in thoughtless content.

> —Julian Moynahan, "The Hero's Guilt: The Case of *Great Expectations*," *Essays in Criticism* 10, No. 1 (January 1960): 77–79

❖

HARRY STONE ON FAIRY-TALE ASPECTS OF *GREAT EXPECTATIONS*

[Harry Stone (b. 1926) has written several books on Dickens, including *Dickens and the Invisible World* (1979) and *The Night Side of Dickens* (1994). In this extract, Stone finds that *Great Expectations* incorporates many aspects of the fairy tale, something Stone believes to be common throughout Dickens's work.]

The magical names of *Great Expectations* and the relationships they mirror or disguise are organic portions of the novel's fairy-tale conception. That conception controls the book again and again. Thus, though Pip fails to marry the true princess in the primary fairy tale, Joe, the true prince, does win her, and so fulfills a minor fairy tale theme. And though Pip's accrual of money proves a curse, Herbert's identical accrual of money (the fairy tale within the fairy tale) proves a blessing—and this not only to Herbert but to Pip. Pip's anonymous endowment of Herbert is the only good that comes of his expectations. By having the identical fairy-tale money given in the identical fairy-tale manner corrupt in one instance and save in the other, Dickens is showing that it is not money itself which corrupts but its improper use—a lesson elaborated by the money-giving of Magwitch and Miss Havisham. All this is so unobtrusively embedded in the action that it comes as something of a shock to discover that the rewards and retributions in *Great Expectations* are as carefully weighted as in the early novels. But now the rewards elaborate and fulfill the theme; in the early novels they wrenched it.

The fairy-tale configurations outlined here are buttressed by hundreds of complementary details. The onset and development of the magical relationship between Magwitch and Pip, for example, gains much from its fairy-tale associations. When Pip meets Magwitch he falls under his spell, a submission accompanied by ritualistic portents. The moment of yielding occurs at the instant Magwitch upends Pip—Magwitch's hypnotic eyes bore "powerfully down" into Pip's, while Pip's innocent eyes look "most helplessly" up into the convict's. In this fateful instant of weakness, Pip yields himself to evil, a yielding marked by a fairy-tale meeting of eyes, the first of many similar looks. Pip's dawning moment of individual identity is also a moment of taint and guilt. His subsequent sense of sinfulness is a realistic reflection of his contamination (a contamination which is really a part of the human condition, which is coeval with individuality and self-consciousness), but his contamination, like his induction, is also underlined by fairy-tale signs. The evil adult world impinges upon Pip in the same way that Dickens, in his own childhood, visualized a sadistic adult world impinging upon himself. The supreme imagery of evil is adapted from the imagery of fairy tales: it involves fateful glances, solemn compacts, ogres, cannibalism, and the like; and in each world the crucial relationship is the same: it centers about a brutal adult and a waiflike child. Yet the effect of the book is neither fabulous nor self-pitying. Dickens avoids the former distortion because his basic situation is psychologically realistic—it emerges from his own experiences; he avoids the latter because, although he surrounds Pip with an expressionistic reflection of his own childhood terror, he distances that terror through retrospective humor. For the reader, therefore, Pip's real but fairy-tale nightmare partakes of fairy-tale whimsey—a combination which allows Dickens to reveal and conceal his involvement.

Magwitch, for instance, threatens to eat Pip's "fat cheeks"—a threat that Pip accepts as literal. Later Magwitch swears to have Pip's heart and liver "tore out, roasted and ate," and he tells the trembling child of a bloodthirsty cohort who can "softly creep and creep his way to him and tear him open"—the exact threat Good Mrs. Brown terrified Florence with in *Dombey and Son.* This ogreish bullying is grotesque and amusing—for Dickens as well as the reader. But for Dickens it also carries a burden of undiminished horror, a burden made explicit by Pip's reactions and their consequences. Pip finds Magwitch's ferocious threats as real and endlessly ramifying as the young Dickens found the atrocities in "Captain Murderer" or "Chips and the Devil"—two blood-thirsty cannibalistic stories that he heard nightly from his nurse. (A key word in the terrorizing refrain of "Chips and the Devil" is "Pips.") As a result of Magwitch's cannibalistic threats, Pip enters into an indissoluble compact to aid him, and Pip's last glimpse of the outlaw occurs as he glances "over his shoulder" while racing homeward toward the forge. In that backward glance (so reminiscent of fateful glances in mythology and fairy lore) Pip sees Magwitch plunging toward the river, the flowing stream which runs symbolically through all of *Great Expectations* and which will ultimately convey Magwitch and himself to death and salvation.

—Harry Stone, "Fire, Hand, and Gate: Dickens' *Great Expectations,*" *Kenyon Review* 24, No. 4 (Autumn 1962): 678–80

♣

[H. M. Daleski (b. 1926) is the author of many critical studies, including *The Forked Flame: A Study of D. H. Lawrence* (1965), *The Divided Heroine* (1984), and *Unities: Studies in the English Novel* (1985). In this extract, taken from his book on Dickens, Daleski examines Dickens's choice of first-person narration in *Great Expectations*, which seems to have caused Dickens to unearth many autobiographical details in the portrayal of Pip.]

Great Expectations is one of Dickens's most personal novels, as personal, perhaps, even as *David Copperfield;* and consequently it bears the marks of his own cravings to an unusual degree. It has generally been held that Pip's passion for Estella, the most strongly expressed passion in the novels to this point, is a reflection of Dickens's feelings for Ellen Ternan; we may add that his relationship with the young actress is furthermore reflected in the emphasis in the novel on hidden relationship. But I would suggest that it was Dickens's decision to use Pip as a first-person narrator that determined the emotional centre of the novel, which is not the relationship of Pip and Estella. For Dickens this decision meant that his new novel would inevitably challenge comparison with *David Copperfield,* the only other work from which he had debarred himself as omniscient author; and to ensure that he did not repeat himself, he read the earlier novel again some six weeks before the first instalment of the new novel appeared: 'To be quite sure I had fallen into no unconscious repetitions, I read *David Copperfield* again the other day, and was affected by it to a degree you would hardly believe.' It seems at least likely that the use of the first-person method and the reading of *David Copperfield* reactivated Dickens's sense of his early traumatic experiences, particularly the sense of being abandoned by both his parents when he was sent to work at the blacking warehouse; and in the incalculable ways of the imagination this led to his unconsciously shaping the plot he had devised into a vehicle for the vicarious satisfaction of his own deepest need as a child. Certainly the matrix of the plot is the abandonment and rejection of children: Pip, the orphan, who has never seen his father and mother and is brought up by hand, has the continued sense as a child of being always treated as if he 'had insisted on being born in opposition to the dictates of reason, religion, and morality, and against the dissuading arguments of [his] best friends'; this is how Magwitch recounts his earliest memory: 'I first become aware of myself, down in Essex, a thieving turnips for my living. Summun had run away from me—a man—a tinker—and he'd took the fire with him, and left me wery cold'; and Estella, as a child, is handed over to Jaggers by her mother, to be done with as he sees fit. We may add that Miss Havisham, though not a child, is abandoned by her lover on her wedding day.

> —H. M. Daleski, *Dickens and the Art of Analogy* (New York: Schocken Books, 1970), pp. 241–42

❖

A. E. Dyson on Magwitch

[A. E. Dyson (b. 1928) is a distinguished British critic and author of *The Crazy Fabric: Essays in Irony* (1965) and, with Julian Lovelock, *Masterful Images: English Poetry form Metaphysicals to Romantics* (1976). He is a former Senior Lecturer in English and American Studies at the University of East Anglia. In this extract, Dyson focuses on the character of Magwitch, whom he believes to be a fundamentally decent individual in spite of his life as a criminal.]

In this devious plot, what if anything can be said for Magwitch, who so disastrously usurps Joe's place as second father to Pip? The small Pip had confided to him the loss of his father—indeed, Pip was attacked on his father's tombstone—so Magwitch at least knows, or thinks he knows, Pip's parental void. Further, he persuades himself that his undertaking is wholly unselfish; he chooses for his adopted son not some new name, as Betsey Trotwood had done for David, but the name 'Pip' that the child had given to himself. Here is an almost humble sense of Pip's identity, which Magwitch will respect, consciously at least, at every turn. There is the further sense that in giving Pip money and status he is rescuing him from his own former predicament, and giving the boy a unique chance of freedom and happiness in life. It must be admitted also that, misreading the young Pip's fear as pity, Magwitch has at least responded to pity with love instead of hate. His project compares not unfavourably with Miss Havisham's plans for Estella. Both adopt a child, and offer education, the one for making a lady, the other a gentleman, after the way of the world. Both are genuinely concerned for the child—in her way Miss Havisham loves Estella—and both use the child in a personal and delusional dream of revenge. But whereas Miss Havisham's 'revenge' is born of hatred, Magwitch's comes from a comparatively innocent pride. Estella is to provide for Miss Havisham the spectacle of males in agony; Pip is merely to charm himself, and society, and so to justify Magwitch's ruined life. The consciousness of for once in his life doing good sustains Magwitch, and helped along with oaths sworn on his pocket Bible, he achieves that most unusual thing in Dickens's novels or, indeed, in life as we know it, a genuine conversion from criminality in his middle age.

At root, it seems, Magwitch has always been decent; and it is part of Dickens's greatness to demonstrate just the psychological spur required to change him to the extent that we see. Yet it hardly needs adding that Magwitch's plan, in the aspects hidden from him, is a terrible violation of Pip, and at exactly that precious point—Pip's identity—which Magwitch thinks he respects. Pip is used as a thing in Magwitch's own strange fight for salvation, and from any perspective outside Magwitch the terrible consequences cry aloud to be seen. But it is of a piece with the delusional mentality that Magwitch cannot see from any other angle; and, moreover, that despite the stringent condition of secrecy laid upon Pip about his benefactor, he is privately convinced that Pip 'must know'. If it is so central to Magwitch's life, how can it be less so to Pip's? The boy will naturally and joyfully have detected his second father from the first.

Dickens nowhere makes these implications explicit, but embodies them in vividly brilliant scenes. They are unmistakeable in Magwitch's manner of revealing himself, and in the tone of affectionate ownership and complicity, unbearable to Pip, which he instinctively adopts. The lesson of Pip's snobbery to Joe, real and painful enough in such a horrible denouement, is one aspect only of a confrontation which Pip's reason barely survives. Little wonder that Pip conceives an almost unconquerable aversion to this man, when even Herbert, unimplicated in Magwitch's wealth (as he fondly believes), shrinks away. Pip's subsequent willingness to detect and honour the goodness in Magwitch's conduct is not a simple recovery from snobbery, but courage of a rare and fine kind. But Pip is dazed by his own misfortunes during this period and enveloped in a nightmare; and when all is finished, he sinks into a fever and almost dies.

> —A. E. Dyson, *The Inimitable Dickens: A Study of the Novels*
> (London: Macmillan, 1970), pp. 238–40

❖

Q. D. LEAVIS ON GUILT AND CLASS IN *GREAT EXPECTATIONS*

[Q. D. Leavis (1906–1981) was an important British literary critic. With her husband, F. R. Leavis, she founded the journal *Scrutiny,* and she also wrote the study *Fiction and the Reading Public* (1932). Her *Collected Essays* began publication in 1983. In this extract, Leavis believes the core of *Great Expectations* to lie in its examination of guilt and class-consciousness.]

Dickens's preoccupations in *Great Expectations* are with the fundamental realities of his society and focus on two questions: how was it that a sense of *guilt* was implanted in every child, and with what consequences? And what part does *Class* play in the development of such a member of that society? The novelist is concerned with the effects of these two sanctions, guilt and shame, and it is an inseparable feature of this concern that he constantly insinuates the question: what is 'real' in such a context? for Pip is continually in doubt and perplexity as to whether the real life is that social one with its rules of right and wrong, into which he was born, or the life of the imagination that grows out of natural feeling, into which he was inducted from the opening chapter, his first distinct memory. Of course it is in the working out and presentation of these inquiries that the value of the novel lies, in the minute particularities of the individual life which are yet so skilfully invented as to carry overtones of allegory and to be exemplary. The pertinacity and concentration of Dickens's mind on his theme has made the two questions, in which the third is implied, so interwoven as to be inseparable eventually, and his Shakespearean genius as a creator has produced the wonderful plot which is not only exciting to read and faultless in execution but strikingly classical in its peripeteia. Every detail of the plot, moreover, expresses some aspect, some further aspect, of the theme, and one that is necessary for its full apprehension by the reader. A remarkable feature of the novel is the complexity of the irony which informs the plot from beginning to end (the rewritten end which is demonstrably superior to the one first intended and which perfectly completes the intention and meaning of the novel)—an irony which inheres in the title; yet the novel is affirmative and constructive, not, like other novels shot through with irony (e.g. *Huckleberry Finn, The Confidence Man, Le Rouge et le Noir*), pessimistic or nihilistic.

And whereas Dickens's difficulties, ever since they first appeared in *Oliver Twist,* in reconciling the reader's demands for realism with his own need, for his creative intentions, of a non-rational symbolism of situation and action, a freer form of dealing with experience than his inheritance from the eighteenth-century novelists provided, he has at last, in *Great Expectations,* managed to reconcile realism and symbolism so that in this novel we move without protest, or uneasiness even, from the 'real' world of everyday experience into the non-rational life of the guilty conscience or spiritual experience, outside time and place and with its own logic: somehow we are inhibited from applying the rules of common sense to it even where we hardly recognize that it is symbolic action and can not possibly be plausible real life. The novel is also remarkable for having no wide divergences of prose style either, as even *Bleak House* has; almost the only rhetoric is the passage where Pip tries to explain to Estella his feelings for her, where the effect of weak egotism is required and deliberately obtained through rhetorical language. There is a consistent sobriety of language without losing idiomatic identity for the characters, who range widely nevertheless, as from Jaggers to Joe, from Wemmick to Herbert, from Miss Havisham to Mrs. Joe, and this personal idiom is even what distinguishes Magwitch from Orlick. While Dickens works here, as in *George Silverman's Explanation,* with the minimum in word, setting and characterization, he does not sacrifice in *Great Expectations* scope, range, richness or imaginative complexity. This is the Dickens novel the mature and exigent are now likely to re-read most often and to find more and more in each time, perhaps because it seems to have more relevance outside its own age than any other of Dickens's creative work.

> —Q. D. Leavis, "How We Must Read *Great Expectations,*" *Dickens the Novelist* by F. R. Leavis and Q. D. Leavis (London: Chatto & Windus, 1970), pp. 288–89

❖

JOHN LUCAS ON PIP AS CHARACTER AND PIP AS NARRATOR

[John Lucas (b. 1937) is a professor of English and drama at the University of Loughborough in Leicestershire, England. He has written *The Literature of Change* (1977), *England and Englishness* (1990), and other works. In this extract, Lucas points out that Pip as narrator has a different point of view than Pip as a character, and that Pip's own judgment of himself may perhaps be unduly harsh.]

There are essentially two points of view in *Great Expectations.* One is that of the Pip who lives through the novel, the other belongs to the Pip who narrates it. And the second point of view is the authoritative one, commenting on, correcting, judging the earlier self (or selves). To take just one example. When Joe accompanies Pip to Miss Havisham's to speak about the boy's being apprenticed, we are told that he will not talk to Miss Havisham but addresses all his remarks to Pip:

> It was quite in vain for me to endeavour to make him sensible
> that he ought to speak to Miss Havisham. The more I made
> faces and gestures to him to do it, the more confidential, argu-
> mentative, and polite, he persisted in being to Me.
>
> 'Have you brought his indentures with you?' asked Miss
> Havisham.
>
> 'Well, Pip, you know,' replied Joe, as if that were a little
> unreasonable, 'you see me put 'em in my 'at, and therefore you
> know as they are here.' With which he took them out, and gave
> them, not to Miss Havisham, but to me. I am afraid I was
> ashamed of the dear good fellow—I *know* I was ashamed of
> him—when I saw that Estella stood at the back of Miss
> Havisham's chair, and that her eyes laughed mischievously. I
> took the indentures out of his hand and gave them to Miss
> Havisham. (ch. 13)

It is a beautifully caught moment. On the one hand there is
the boy's genuine and even perhaps excusable embarrassment.
On the other, there is the narrator's self-accusation. And the
fineness of the scene—its truth—depends on the way that the
acknowledgement of shame is handled. 'I am afraid I was
ashamed of the dear good fellow.' That is not shame. It has
about it the clear hint of condescension which appeals to the
reader to understand that there was every reason for shame.
And of course Pip, the man who is launched into society, *does*
feel superior to his country relatives, there is no helping it. But
there is every helping the self-knowledge that can pass into
self-congratulation. Hence the stern—'I *know* I was ashamed of
him.' The qualification acts as a rebuke to the previous lightly
accepted culpability. It shows that the narrator is determined to
get at the real truth.

I have made heavy weather of what is a fairly simple matter.
Yet it is worth emphasizing how sternly Pip wishes to judge
himself and his life. All signs of self-pity and complacency are
rooted out as they become identified.

But this brings us to an interesting point. The severity of Pip's
self-judgement may eventually prove to be in excess of what
he has to show us of his life. In other words, there is a third
point of view that *Great Expectations* allows for—ours. Almost
the best thing about the novel is that because of the self-exco-
riating quality with which Pip is determined to tell the truth
about himself, we understand that his desire to atone for past

errors leads him to identify error where none exists. There must be no hint of a desire for martyrdom about this, or the novel will be ruined. Dickens's success depends on his making Pip's desire for atonement plausible and honourable, not priggish or coy. And by and large the success is guaranteed because in spite of Pip's faults we are persuaded of his honesty, candour and essential likeability. Because, although it is proper that *he* should regard the course of his life as dictated by faults, it is also proper that we should see the matter otherwise. In particular, the novel makes us understand that great expectations are highly problematic. Can one even be guilty of entertaining them, or are they inevitably fed into people's lives?

—John Lucas, *The Melancholy Man: A Study of Dickens's Novels* (London: Methuen, 1970), pp. 290–92

❧

PEARL CHESLER SOLOMON ON DICKENS AND HIS FATHER

[Pearl Chesler Solomon is a professor of teacher education at St. Thomas Aquinas College in Sparkill, New York, and author of *Dickens and Melville in Their Time* (1975), from which the following extract is taken. Here, Solomon examines the shift of focus in Dickens's work from *David Copperfield* to *Great Expectations,* noting that in the interval Dickens has come to terms with his feelings for his own father.]

Sometime after his father's death, Dickens said of him, "The longer I live, the better man I think him." In the fragment of autobiography written long before John Dickens's death, Dickens blamed his father's neglect of himself on two faults, ease of temper and straitness of means, and as long as his father lived, Dickens continued to be annoyed by the consequences of these traits. But in *Great Expectations* ease of temper and straitness of means are not incompatible with great virtue. They are, in fact, attributes of the saintly man who was Pip's first father, Joe Gargery. Joe's passivity and poverty in no way harm the child, while his love and protection save him.

Dickens seems to be saying now that the blacking warehouse was not the central crisis of his childhood as the blacksmith's forge was not the central crisis of Pip's. The crisis of Pip's childhood has nothing to do with money or class, but with love. Pip's hell is the absence of love, and it is the sister who takes the place of his mother, and who bears his mother's name, who makes that hell. In some such way as this, Dickens reassessed the events of his own past to make the father his deliverer, his mother his would-be destroyer. The central issue in this reconsideration of his past is, again, the source of love. It was love that saved Pip from Magwitch's fate: his father's love, Joe Gargery's.

So bent is Dickens upon making the principal source of Pip's guilt his criminal ingratitude toward Joe that he entirely removes David's reason for feeling guilty toward his father— the desire he felt for possession of his mother. Pip cannot feel desire for Mrs. Joe, whose embattled bosom, stuck full of pins, repels the advance of all living creatures. It is Joe's second wife who is like Clara Copperfield; who is young and gentle and loving; and who is the object of Orlick's (and therefore of Pip's) lust. But Pip represses his lust for Biddy—is not guilty of even fantasy incest with the woman who will become Joe's wife. And toward the child of Biddy and Joe, the child who is also named Pip, the older Pip will see Joe free to become a better father—the father Mrs. Joe prevented Joe from being to him.

Pip's redemption begins when he realizes that he must renounce Magwitch's money partly because it now seems to him criminal to live on unearned money, partly because, in some narrowly moralistic way, Pip doesn't deserve it. But there is a sense in which Pip doesn't get Magwitch's money because he deserves something better than a criminal's patrimony. By means of Pip's association with Magwitch, Dickens is reassessing once more the blacking warehouse experience. It is through Magwitch and Magwitch's money that Pip is dragged to the borderline of the criminal underworld, and Pip must reject both the man and his money in order to remain a "gentleman." What Pip has *earned* from Magwitch, Dickens seems to feel, is the right to respectable employment. What he has been given unearned, again, is an education. And it is this education which was Magwitch's gift to him, along with the unearned love which was Joe's gift, which together "fathered" Pip, and which made of him a true gentleman.

—Pearl Chesler Solomon, *Dickens and Melville in Their Time* (New York: Columbia University Press, 1975), pp. 168–71

❖

MURRAY BAUMGARTEN ON WRITING AND SPEECH IN *GREAT EXPECTATIONS*

[Murray Baumgarten is a professor of general literature at the University of California at Santa Cruz. He has written *City Scriptures: Modern Jewish Writing* (1982) and *Understanding Philip Roth* (1990). In this extract, Baumgarten studies *Great Expectations* in the context of Dickens's stenographic activities as a reporter, showing that these activities helped to break down the distinction between writing speech in Dickens's mind and in the minds of his readers.]

By the time he published *Great Expectations* in serial form in 1860–1861, Dickens had already written twelve novels, edited four magazines for which he had written at least a million words, and published two books of travel and social observation. He was forty-nine years old.

He began his career as a court reporter and transcriber of Parliamentary debates, which he reproduced for newspaper publication with phenomenal speed and accuracy. Like Pip, Dickens had taught himself to read and write; like David Copperfield he had taught himself to take shorthand before he was sixteen, very quickly becoming the best stenographer of his time. As Steven Marcus points out in a classic article, this talent of Dickens' helped make it possible for him to recast the conventional relation between speech and writing.

Once he had mastered the stenographic characters in a process that receives brilliant description in Chapter 38 of *David Copperfield,* they were no longer the constituents of an imprisoning code, Marcus points out, but the playful doodles of speech. The stenographic "characters, as he describes them in recollection, were themselves doodles—apparently random plays of the pen, out of which figures or partial figures would emerge and to which meaning could be ascribed." As a result, speech could "now be rendered not only in the abstract forms of cursive or printed letters and units; it could be represented *graphically* as well." Marcus emphasizes that this "experience of an alternative, quasi-graphic way of representing speech had among other things the effect upon Dickens of loosening up the rigid relations between speech and writing that prevail in our linguistic and cultural system." These flourishes of the pen, these squiggles and doodles, provided Dickens "with an experience of something that closely resembled a hieroglyphic means of preserving speech," making it possible for "the spoken language to enter into his writing with a parity it had never enjoyed before in English fictional prose. Speech here was not the traditional subordinate of its written representation; it could appear now in writing with a freedom and spontaneity that made it virtually, if momentarily, writing's equal." Dramatizing the acquisition of literacy in *Great Expectations,* and revealing the gulf between oral and written culture, Dickens occupies a particularly heady moment in western cultural history. He can look both ways, and bring into the future alphabetic code of the west the childhood experience of calligraphy, when the alphabetic character is both phoneme and picture.

In this novel as was the case throughout the nineteenth century, most reading was reading aloud; then writing must be the (sometimes) private act of making the characters that provide a public voice. Perhaps the act of decoding in which we are engaged parallel to that of the characters of *Great Expectations* will lead us as well to the greater magic of encoding—so that we like them may inscribe our selves in the world in which they too are circumscribed. Then our story would become more than a private possession, and be changed into public meaning. Like money that Wemmick refers to as portable property, our story would have added to the store of language and become something from which, like capital, we could all benefit.

Reading *Great Expectations* aloud, we become one of its community of readers. We are the witnesses to its experience.

As Pip speaks to us we are not imprisoned in the code of reading, but rather liberated by calligraphic impulses; the characters of the novel, both alphabetic and fictive, are writ large as our meaning. We envision the scene, encounter the portrayed situation, and believe in this rendered world, for it is a true story. In referring to Marcus, I do not mean to make *Great Expectations* into an avatar of *Pickwick Papers*. Rather, it is to emphasize that our experience in reading this novel is not just Pip's deciphering of a code—not mere transcription—but the rhythm of participating in its production. Thereby, we share in a particular version of calligraphic experience. *Great Expectations* gives writing the qualities of speech, the flow of language unceasing and unending. We are sorry when it stops.

—Murray Baumgarten, "Calligraphy and Code: Writing in *Great Expectations*," *Dickens Studies Annual* 11 (1983): 69–70

❧

Thomas Loe on the Gothic Elements in *Great Expectations*

[Thomas Loe is a professor of English at the State University of New York College at Oswego. In this extract, Loe believes that *Great Expectations* is an amalgam of three types of novel: the *Bildungsroman,* or the novel of development from childhood to adulthood; the novel of manners; and the Gothic novel of terror and the supernatural. Loe focuses on this third type, drawing parallels between Dickens's work and Ann Radcliffe's *The Italian* (1797).]

The Gothic novel plot of *The Italian* fits the literal circumstances of the action of *Great Expectations* very closely, and, even though subdued by the *Bildungsroman* and novel of manners plots that dominate the first two stages of Pip's story, this plot initiates the action of the novel and emerges in the final stage to unify and conclude the novel. Some specific parallels could even be argued to exist between the two novels if not pressed too far: Pip resembles both the persecuted Ellena and Vivaldi in his passivity and innocence; Miss Havisham, in her dedication to revenge, resembles the plotting Marchesa; Magwitch and Schedoni have similar roles as accomplices to Compeyson and Nicola, and their ultimate exposures of one another and their deaths are also similar; both books have henchmen like Orlick and Spalatro, who figure in the final explanations about the suspicions of persecution that permeate the novels; and Estella's relationship as daughter to Magwitch is very much like the father-daughter relationship thought to exist between Ellena and Schedoni. The most important structural similarity, though, is the way crime and two shadowy criminals, Nicola and Compeyson, lurk in the backgrounds of the plots in both novels. In *Great Expectations* these archvillains function as they do for the Gothic novel in general: they provide memorable, smoothly coherent actions by allowing the malignant effect of an original evil to be traced through cliff-hanging interruptions. Crime, the manifestation of this evil, is the major metaphor of this plot for all Gothic novels. "That evil genius" (ch. 50) Compeyson, despite his only occasional, furtive presence, is the emblematic character for crime and the prime mover of the Gothic plot which eventually ties together all the major lines of action in *Great Expectations*.

So, although Compeyson and his crimes have been taken to task by critics because they are obscure in the first two thirds of the novel and then blatant and melodramatic, it is from their very obscurity that they derive their forcefulness and eventual dominance in the structure of the novel. Dickens begins the action with the intrusion of Magwitch and Compeyson into the formative starting point of Pip's life, his "first most vivid and broad impression of the identity of things" (ch. 1), which becomes interwoven with the images of crime, convicts, guilt, and terror which characterize his narrative. Magwitch and Miss Havisham, as well as Estella, Pip, and Jaggers, are important participants in this hidden Gothic plot, and even Orlick's mysterious behind-the-scenes actions are enveloped in his associations of Compeyson. The effect of Pip's imagination working on the associations he has with Orlick, for example, heighten his reaction to the glimpses and reports of a "lurker" he gets (ch. 40; ch. 43) prowling around his lodgings. This response parallels and presages the more awful "terror" generated later by the presence of Compeyson, who is revealed by Mr. Wopsle to have sat behind Pip in the theater: "I cannot exaggerate the enhanced disquiet into which this conversation threw me, or the special and peculiar terror I felt as Compeyson's having been behind me 'like a ghost' " (ch. 47). The "special and peculiar" effect is created largely because it is a secret and internalized one. It is an interior effect, a psychological one, created by an imaginative reaction to events, rather than the actual events themselves. Robert Heilman has shown how the similar Gothic accoutrements of *Jane Eyre* create an internalized heightened response in that novel. This same principle of obscurity, so skillfully utilized by Ann Radcliffe, employs Pip's internalized fears to create links between the various plots in *Great Expectations.* Compeyson's crimes against Miss Havisham and Magwitch are created before the time that the novel opens, and the consequences that are visited upon Pip and Estella by their distorted donors are greatly removed from the times and scenes of the crime itself. It is these removed actions that have to be sorted out retrospectively, making the gothic plot resemble a detective plot.

From a retrospective perspective the Gothic plot appears straight-forward, like the evil behind it. It consists of Pip's initial help to Magwitch and Magwitch's subsequent attempt to play patron to Pip. Magwitch tries to revenge himself against the society he feels is responsible for his criminal fall and subsequent prosecution, linked in his mind with Compeyson. The parallel plot of Estella is created by Miss Havisham in revenge against men for being deserted by Compeyson. Both plot motivations are bound tightly with Compeyson's evil. Although overlaid in the first two thirds of the novel by the *Bildungsroman* plot and the novel of manners plot, the Gothic plot is kept active by interspersed, brief, but important, reminders of its presence, such as the man stirring his rum-and-water with a file (ch. 10) or the later indirect encounter with this same emissary on a stage coach (ch. 28). Fear-inspiring Gothic imagery connected with death, decay, violence, and mental distortions support such actions, and foreshadow the eruption of the Gothic plot with Magwitch's appearance in Chapter Thirty-nine, in what Pip calls "the turning point of my life" (ch. 37).

Locating the stories and motivations and sorting out the connections between Compeyson, Magwitch, Miss Havisham, Arthur Havisham, and Jaggers make up the rest of the Gothic plot. These correspond generally with the separate plot lines that are played off against one another by creating expectations for the reader, and then interrupted with another story. Even though the plotting and actions leading up to the final river flight and its aftermath are often regarded as "one of the highest achievements of the sensation novel" (Lionel Stevenson), they are integrally bound with the deliberate obscurity of the main Gothic plot that flows, subdued or dominant, throughout the novel. What has been deliberately concealed is finally revealed for maximum effect. This third type of plot is also bound closely with the change of heart that Pip has towards Magwitch, the last important development of his *Bildungsroman* plot, and with the concurrent collapse of his social aspirations inspired by his idealization of Estella, the motivation behind the novel of manners plot.

—Thomas Loe, "Gothic Plot in *Great Expectations,*" *Dickens Quarterly* 6, No. 3 (September 1989): 107–9

❖

GAIL TURLEY HOUSTON ON THE ABSENCE OF A MOTHER FIGURE IN PIP'S LIFE

[Gail Turley Houston (b. 1950) is a professor of English at Brigham Young University (Provo, Utah) and the author of *Consuming Fictions: Gender, Class, and Hunger in Dickens's Novels* (1994), from which the following extract is taken. Here, Houston maintains that Pip's lack of a mother figure in his life results in his becoming the victim of market forces.]

Being raised "by hand," referring to the laborious and usually unsuccessful practice of feeding orphans or abandoned infants by hand rather than by bringing in a wet nurse, signifies Pip's physical deprivation of the breast in the primal infantine stage, but it also implies his deprivation of maternal love. Given her brother's fragile beginnings, the woman who raised him "by hand," Mrs. Joe, ironically believes that Pip should not be "Pompeyed," that is, pampered; of course, being raised "by hand" comes to refer to Mrs. Joe's physical abuse of her brother. Furthermore, Mrs. Joe also expects remuneration for having raised Pip "by hand," for obviously she hopes to advance her own fortunes by placing him at Miss Havisham's disposal. Her ally, Pumblechook, co-opts the phrase, and, by acknowledging that his niece raised Pip by hand, gives added weight to his own claim that he is Pip's mentor in economic terms (and thus deserving of Pip's newly inherited "Capital" when he ludicrously suggests that he "made" Pip. Likewise, Pip thinks and hopes that "Miss Havisham was going to make my fortune on a grand scale," but he is repulsed that he is the gentleman Magwitch has " 'made' " and " 'owns.' "

Fallen into the world of production and consumption, Pip is not born, he is made, and that makes him particularly vulnerable to the cannibalistic world of Victorian England. James E. Marlow suggests that for the reader of *Great Expectations* "the dread of being eaten structures the novel." Asserting that after 1859 "the themes of orality, predation, and the translation of human flesh into economic gain—all metaphoric cannibalism— dominate [Dickens'] fiction," Marlow argues that by this point Dickens believed that cannibalism was not just an "aberration" in ogres like Quilp but rather "a custom sanctioned by the ideologues of capitalism" such as Merdle and Casby. Given the paradigm I use to study Dickens's fiction, in *Great Expectations* production displaces reproduction whenever the individual is abandoned or betrayed by family, particularly by the mother.

With no nourishing mother figure, Pip becomes the object of market relations, learning only to consume or be consumed. Once again, Dickens's representation of such consumption is graphic and ludicrously literal: his descriptions of Pip's rise to and fall from fortune center on the gluttony and starvation that oscillate in Pip as his often violent assertion of hunger conflicts with his sense of being devoured. In his "first most vivid and broad impression of the identity of things," a convict threatens to eat Pip if he does not bring him food and a file. As Magwitch later explains to Pip, he turned to crime because he was starving and no one ever " 'measured my stomach,' " for " 'I must put something into my stomach, mustn't I?' " When asked what his occupation is, the convict replies, " 'Eat and drink . . . if you'll find the materials.' " However, eating and drinking in a society that tolerates physical or emotional starvation may be defined as robbery, and Dickens does seem to suggest that any kind of market relations between human beings is robbery, or, worse, cannibalism. Thus, Pip becomes like the convict: the starving child of his sister's bad breast, he broods "I was going to rob Mrs. Joe," and he metaphorically assaults the surrogate mother's unreproductive breast by invading his sister's pantry.

But as Marlow suggests, the scene that follows indicates that "Pip's dread of being eaten was established long before the arrival of Magwitch." Like Oliver Twist, young Pip seems in constant danger of being eaten by adult swine. In the Christmas Day feasting scene, so much like the Christmas Day scene in *The Pickwick Papers,* tales of the eating or dissection of children act as appetizers for the adults. Wopsle begins the linguistic cannibalism:

> "Swine," pursued Mr. Wopsle, in his deepest voice, and pointing his fork at my blushes, as if he were mentioning my christian name, "Swine were the companions of the prodigal. The gluttony of Swine is put before us, as an example to the young." (I thought this pretty well in him who had been praising up the pork for being so plump and juicy.) "What is detestable in a pig, is more detestable in a boy."

Pumblechook takes up the sermon, focusing on the "boy," Pip. He opines, " 'If you'd been born a Squeaker,' " which Mrs. Joe heartily affirms he was, " 'you would have been disposed of for so many shillings according to the market price of the article, and Dunstable the butcher . . . would have shed your blood and had your life.' " The suggestion is, and Marlow alludes to it as well, that Pip's relations with his sister and her uncle are "market" relations, their chief interest in him being both what fortune they can accrue through him and what repayment they may make him give them for how much effort and energy they have spent in raising him. To extend the metaphor, in a later scene Joe clumsily remarks of Pip's London apartments, " 'I wouldn't keep a pig in it myself—not in the case that I wished him to fatten wholesome and to eat with a meller flavour on him.' " This remarkable statement by the "angel" of the novel suggests just how much Pip is consumable " 'property,' " subject to the market and its consuming practices.

—Gail Turley Houston, *Consuming Fictions: Gender, Class, and Hunger in Dickens's Novels* (Carbondale: Southern Illinois University Press, 1994), pp. 163–65

❖

Books by
Charles Dickens

Sketches by "Boz," Illustrative of Every-day Life and Every-day People. 1836. 2 vols.

Sunday under Three Heads. 1836.

The Village Coquettes: A Comic Opera. 1836.

The Posthumous Papers of the Pickwick Club. 1836–37. 20 parts.

The Strange Gentleman: A Comic Burletta. 1837.

Memoirs of Joseph Grimaldi (editor). 1838. 2 vols.

Sketches of Young Gentlemen. 1838.

Oliver Twist; or, The Parish Boy's Progress. 1838. 3 vols.

The Life and Adventures of Nicholas Nickleby. 1838–39. 20 parts.

The Loving Ballad of Lord Bateman (with William Makepeace Thackeray). 1839.

Sketches of Young Couples. 1840.

Master Humphrey's Clock ⟨The Old Curiosity Shop; Barnaby Rudge⟩. 1840–41. 88 parts.

The Pic Nic Papers (editor). 1841. 3 vols.

American Notes. 1842. 2 vols.

A Christmas Carol in Prose: Being a Ghost-Story of Christmas. 1843.

The Life and Adventures of Martin Chuzzlewit, His Relatives, Friends and Enemies. 1843–44. 20 parts.

The Chimes: A Goblin Story of Some Bells That Rang an Old Year Out and a New Year In. 1845.

The Cricket on the Hearth: A Fairy Tale of Home. 1846.

Pictures from Italy. 1846.

The Battle of Life: A Love Story. 1846.

Dealings with the Firm of Dombey and Son Wholesale, Retail and for Exportation. 1846–48. 20 parts.

An Appeal to Fallen Women. 1847.

Works. 1847–67. 17 vols.

The Haunted Man and the Ghost's Bargain: A Fancy for Christmas Time. 1848.

Elegy Written in a Country Churchyard. c. 1849.

The Personal History, Adventures, Experiences and Observations of David Copperfield the Younger. 1849–50. 20 parts.

Mr. Nightingale's Diary: A Farce (with Mark Lemon). 1851.

Bleak House. 1852–53. 20 parts.

A Child's History of England. 1852–54. 3 vols.

Hard Times, for These Times. 1854.

Speech Delivered at the Meeting of the Administrative Reform Association. 1855.

Little Dorrit. 1855–57. 20 parts.

Novels and Tales Reprinted from Household Words (editor). 1856–59. 11 vols.

The Case of the Reformers in the Literary Fund (with others). 1858.

Speech at the Anniversary Festival of the Hospital for Sick Children. 1858.

Speech at the First Festival Dinner of the Playground and Recreation Society. 1858.

Works (Library Edition). 1858–59 (22 vols.), 1861–74 (30 vols.).

A Tale of Two Cities. 1859. 8 parts.

Christmas Stories from Household Words. 1859. 9 parts.

Great Expectations. 1861. 3 vols.

Great Expectations: A Drama. 1861.

The Uncommercial Traveller. 1861.

An Address on Behalf of the Printer's Pension Society. c. 1864.

Speech at the North London or University College Hospital: Anniversary Dinner in Aid of the Funds. 1864.

Our Mutual Friend. 1864–65. 20 parts.

The Frozen Deep (with Wilkie Collins). 1866.

No Thoroughfare (with Wilkie Collins). 1867.

Speech at the Railway Benevolent Institution: Ninth Annual Dinner. 1867.

Works (Charles Dickens Edition). 1867–75. 21 vols.

Christmas Stories from All the Year Round. c. 1868. 9 parts.

The Readings of Mr. Charles Dickens, as Condensed by Himself. 1868.

Address Delivered at the Birmingham and Midland Institute. 1869.

A Curious Dance round a Curious Tree (with W. H. Wills). 1870.

Speech at Chairman of the Anniversary Festival Dinner of the Royal Free Hospital. 1870.

The Mystery of Edwin Drood. 1870. 6 parts.

Speeches Literary and Social. Ed. R. H. Shepherd. 1870.

The Newsvendors' Benevolent and Provident Institution: Speeches in Behalf of the Institution. 1871.

Is She His Wife? or Something Singular: A Comic Burletta. c. 1872.

The Lamplighter: A Farce. 1879.

The Mudfog Papers, etc. 1880.

Letters. Ed. Georgina Hogarth and Mary Dickens. 1880–82. 3 vols.

Plays and Poems, with a Few Miscellanies in Prose Now First Collected. Ed. R. H. Shepherd. 1885. 2 vols.

The Lazy Tour of Two Idle Apprentices; No Thoroughfare; The Perils of Certain English Prisoners (with Wilkie Collins). 1890.

Works (Macmillan Edition). 1892–1925. 21 vols.

Letters to Wilkie Collins 1851–1870. Ed. Lawrence Hutton. 1892.

Works (Gadshill Edition). Ed. Andrew Lang. 1897–1908. 36 vols.

To Be Read at Dusk and Other Stories, Sketches and Essays. Ed. F. G. Kitton. 1898.

Christmas Stories from Household Words *and* All the Year Round. 1898. 5 vols.

Works (Biographical Edition). Ed. Arthur Waugh. 1902–03. 19 vols.

Poems and Verses. Ed. F. G. Kitton. 1903.

Works (National Edition). Ed. Bertram W. Matz. 1906–08. 40 vols.

Dickens and Maria Beadnell: Private Correspondence. Ed. G. P. Baker. 1908.

The Dickens-Kolle Letters. Ed. Harry B. Smith. 1910.

Works (Centenary Edition). 1910–11. 36 vols.

Dickens as Editor: Letters Written by Him to William Henry Wills, His Sub-Editor. Ed. R. C. Lehmann. 1912.

Works (Waverley Edition). 1913–18. 30 vols.

Unpublished Letters to Mark Lemon. Ed. Walter Dexter. 1927.

Letters to the Baroness Burdett-Coutts. Ed. Charles C. Osborne. 1931.

Dickens to His Oldest Friend: The Letters of a Lifetime to Thomas Beard. Ed. Walter Dexter. 1932.

Letters to Charles Lever. Ed. Flora V. Livingston. 1933.

Mr. and Mrs. Charles Dickens: His Letters to Her. Ed. Walter Dexter. 1935.

The Love Romance of Dickens, Told in His Letters to Maria Beadnell (Mrs. Winter). Ed. Walter Dexter. 1936.

The Nonesuch Dickens. Ed. Arthur Waugh, Hugh Walpole, Walter Dexter, and Thomas Hatton. 1937–38. 23 vols.

Letters. Ed. Walter Dexter. 1938. 3 vols.

The New Oxford Illustrated Dickens. 1947–58. 21 vols.

Speeches. Ed. K. J. Fielding, 1960, 1988.

Letters (Pilgrim Edition). Ed. Madeline House, Graham Storey, Kathleen Tillotson et al. 1965– .

The Clarendon Dickens. Ed. John Butt, Kathleen Tillotson, and James Kinsley. 1966– .

Uncollected Writings from Household Words *1850–1859.* Ed. Harry Stone. 1968.

Complete Plays and Selected Poems. 1970.

Dickens in Europe: Essays. Ed. Rosalind Vallance. 1975.

The Public Readings. Ed. Phillip Collins. 1975.

Supernatural Short Stories. Ed. Michael Hayes. 1978.

The Annotated Dickens. Ed. Edward Giuliano and Philip Collins. 1986. 2 vols.

Dickens' Working Notes for His Novels. Ed. Harry Stone. 1987.

Sketches by Boz and Other Early Papers 1833–39. Ed. Michael Slater. 1994.

Works about Charles Dickens and Great Expectations

Ackroyd, Peter. *Dickens.* New York: HarperCollins, 1990.

Allingham, Philip V. "Patterns of Deception in *Huckleberry Finn* and *Great Expectations.*" *Nineteenth-Century Literature* 46 (1991–92): 447–72.

Barnard, Robert. *Imagery and Theme in the Novels of Dickens.* Oslo: Universitetsforlaget, 1974.

Barzilai, Shuli. "Dickens's *Great Expectations:* The Motive for Moral Masochism." *American Imago* 42 (1985): 45–68.

Bloom, Harold, ed. *Charles Dickens.* New York: Chelsea House, 1987.

Bradbury, Nicola. *Charles Dickens'* Great Expectations. New York: St. Martin's Press, 1990.

Brook, George L. *The Language of Dickens.* London: Andre Deutsch, 1970.

Brooks, Peter. *Reading for the Plot: Design and Intention in Narrative.* Cambridge, MA: Harvard University Press, 1984.

Brown, Carolyn. "*Great Expectations:* Masculinity and Modernity." *Essays and Studies* 40 (1987): 60–74.

Butt, John, and Kathleen Tillotson. *Dickens at Work.* London; Chatto & Windus, 1958.

Carlisle, Janice. *The Sense of an Audience: Dickens, Thackeray, and George Eliot at Mid-Century.* Athens: University of Georgia Press, 1981.

Cheadle, Brian. "Sentiment and Resentment in *Great Expectations.*" *Dickens Studies Annual* 20 (1991): 149–74.

Cockshut, A. O. J. *The Imagination of Charles Dickens.* New York: New York University Press, 1962.

Cohen, William A. "Manual Conduct in *Great Expectations.*" *ELH* 60 (1993): 217–59.

Collins, Philip. *Dickens and Crime.* London: Macmillan, 1962.

Coolidge, Archibald C., Jr. *Charles Dickens as Serial Novelist.* Ames: Iowa State University Press, 1967.

Cotsell, Michael, ed. *Critical Essays on Charles Dickens's* Great Expectations. Boston: G. K. Hall, 1990.

Crawford, Iain. "Pip and the Monster: The Joys of Bondage." *Studies in English Literature 1500–1900* 28 (1988): 625–48.

Cunningham, John. "Christian Allusion, Comedic Structure and the Metaphor of Baptism in *Great Expectations.*" *South Atlantic Review* 59, No. 2 (May 1994): 35–51.

Dabney, Ross. *Love and Property in the Novels of Charles Dickens.* Berkeley: University of California Press, 1967.

Daldry, Graham. *Charles Dickens and the Form of the Novel.* Totowa, NJ: Barnes & Noble, 1987.

Dessner, Lawrence Jay. "*Great Expectations:* 'The Ghost of a Man's Own Father.'" *PMLA* 91 (1976): 436–49.

Dobie, Ann B. "Early Stream-of-Consciousness Writing: *Great Expectations.*" *Nineteenth-Century Fiction* 25 (1970–71): 405–16.

Fielding, K. J. *Charles Dickens: A Critical Introduction.* London: Longmans, Green, 1958.

Garis, Robert E. *The Dickens Theatre: A Reassessment of the Novels.* Oxford: Clarendon Press, 1965.

Gold, Joseph. *Charles Dickens: Radical Moralist.* Minneapolis: University of Minnesota Press, 1972.

Goldberg, Michael. *Carlyle and Dickens.* Athens: University of Georgia Press, 1972.

Gross, John, and Gabriel Pearson, ed. *Dickens and the Twentieth Century.* London: Routledge & Kegan Paul, 1962.

Guérard, Albert J. *The Triumph of the Novel: Dickens, Dostoevsky, Faulkner.* New York: Oxford University Press, 1976.

Hardy, Barbara. *The Moral Art of Dickens.* New York: Oxford University Press, 1970.

Herst, Beth F. *The Dickens Hero: Selfhood and Alienation in the Dickens World.* New York: AMS Press, 1990.

Holbrook, David. *Charles Dickens and the Image of Woman.* New York: New York University Press, 1993.

Hollington, Michael. *Dickens and the Grotesque.* Totowa, NJ: Barnes & Noble, 1984.

Hornback, Bert G. Great Expectations: *A Novel of Friendship.* Boston: Twayne, 1987.

———. *"Noah's Arkitecture": A Study of Dickens's Mythology.* Athens: Ohio University Press, 1972.

House, Humphrey. *The Dickens World.* 2nd ed. London: Oxford University Press, 1961.

Hutter, Albert D. "Crime and Fantasy in *Great Expectations.*" In *Psychoanalysis and Literary Process,* ed. Frederick Crews. Cambridge, MA: Winthrop, 1970, pp. 25–65.

Ingham, Patricia. *Dickens, Women, and Language.* Toronto: University of Toronto Press, 1992.

Johnson, Edgar H. *Charles Dickens: His Tragedy and Triumph.* Rev. ed. London: Allen Lane, 1977.

Kaplan, Fred. *Dickens: A Biography.* New York: Morrow, 1988.

Kincaid, James R. *Dickens and the Rhetoric of Laughter.* Oxford: Clarendon Press, 1971.

Kucich, John. "Action in the Dickens Ending: *Bleak House* and *Great Expectations.*" *Nineteenth-Century Fiction* 33 (1978–79): 88–109.

Leavis, L. R. "The Dramatic Narrator in *Great Expectations.*" *English Studies* 68 (1987): 236–48.

Lettis, Richard. *The Dickens Aesthetic.* New York: AMS Press, 1989.

Manning, Sylvia Bank. *Dickens as Satirist.* New Haven: Yale University Press, 1971.

Meckier, Jerome. "Charles Dickens's *Great Expectations:* A Defense of the Second Ending." *Studies in the Novel* 25 (1993): 28–58.

Miller, J. Hillis. *The Form of Victorian Fiction*. Notre Dame, IN: University of Notre Dame Press, 1970.

Miyoshi, Masao. *The Divided Self: A Perspective on the Literature of the Victorians*. New York: New York University Press, 1969.

Monod, Sylvère. *Dickens the Novelist*. Norman: University of Oklahoma Press, 1968.

Morgan, Nicholas H. *Secret Journeys: Theory and Practice in Reading Dickens*. Rutherford, NJ: Fairleigh Dickinson University Press, 1992.

Newcomb, Mildred. *The Imagined World of Charles Dickens*. Columbus: Ohio State University Press, 1989.

Nisbet, Ada, and Blake Nevius, ed. *Dickens Centennial Essays*. Berkeley: University of California Press, 1971.

Orwell, George. "Charles Dickens." In Orwell's *Dickens, Dali, and Others: Studies in Popular Culture*. New York: Reynal & Hitchcock, 1946, pp. 1–75.

Page, Norman. *A Dickens Companion*. London: Macmillan, 1984.

Partlow, Robert B., Jr., ed. *Dickens the Craftsman: Strategies of Presentation*. Carbondale: Southern Illinois University Press, 1970.

Raina, Badri. *Dickens and the Dialectic of Growth*. Madison: University of Wisconsin Press, 1986.

Sadoff, Dianne F. *Monsters of Affection: Dickens, Eliot and Brontë on Fatherhood*. Baltimore: Johns Hopkins University Press, 1982.

Sadrin, Anny. *Parentage and Inheritance in the Novels of Charles Dickens*. Cambridge, MA: Harvard University Press, 1994.

Schad, John. *The Reader in the Dickensian Mirror: Some New Language*. New York: St. Martin's Press, 1992.

Schwarzbach, F. W. *Dickens and the City*. London: Athlone Press, 1979.

Scott, P. J. M. *Reality and Comic Confidence in Charles Dickens.*
London: Macmillan, 1979.

Slater, Michael, ed. *Dickens 1970: Centenary Essays.* London:
Chapman & Hall, 1970.

Stewart, Garrett. *Dickens and the Trials of Imagination.*
Cambridge, MA: Harvard University Press, 1974.

Stone, Harry. *Dickens and the Invisible World: Fairy Tales,
Fantasy, and Novel-Making.* Bloomington: Indiana University
Press, 1979.

———. *The Night Side of Dickens: Cannibalism, Passion,
Necessity.* Columbus: Ohio State University Press, 1994.

Sucksmith, Harvey Peter. *The Narrative Art of Charles Dickens.*
Oxford: Clarendon Press, 1970.

Thurley, Geoffrey. *The Dickens Myth: Its Genesis and Structure.*
London: Routledge & Kegan Paul, 1976.

Vogel, Jane. *Allegory in Dickens.* Tuscaloosa: University of
Alabama Press, 1977.

Welsh, Alexander. *The City of Dickens.* Oxford: Clarendon
Press, 1971.

———. *From Copyright to Copperfield: The Identity of Dickens.*
Cambridge, MA: Harvard University Press, 1987.

Westburg, Barry. *The Confessional Fictions of Charles Dickens.*
DeKalb: Northern Illinois University Press, 1977.

Williams, Raymond. *The English Novel: From Dickens to
Lawrence.* London: Chatto & Windus, 1970.

Index of
Themes and Ideas